The Acts of Jesus

Copyright 2012 by Warren Lathem

ISBN 978-1-105-60176-7

JRJ Publishing
Lathemtown, GA

Dr. Warren Lathem

2865 Hightower Rd.
Ball Ground, GA 30107
warrenlathem@gmail.com
770 889 6423
www.venezuelaforchrist.blogspot.com

From the author...

Anytime one puts words to paper and places them in view of the public, it is with a mixture of arrogance and humility. Who am I to say anything I think or write is worthy of another's time and interest? At the same time, I must think something here is of value to me and possibly others or it would not be published and put before you, the reader.

Therefore, I am genuinely touched that you would take the time to read even this much. I hope you will read further. However, my primary desire is for the Holy Spirit to take the Word of God exposed in each chapter and use it to touch and comfort and convict your heart – whatever the Holy Spirit desires to do with the sword of the Spirit. If my words can also be used by the Spirit, then I am even more thankful and amazed.

These chapters consist of various sermons preached at Mount Pisgah and Due West United Methodist Churches, as well as several places in Venezuela and have been re-written and revised several times over the last 13 years. One of them was written over 30 years ago and I still have opportunity to share the Good News of the Gospel through the word of God revealed to me in that sermon. I hope they are helpful.

The Acts of Jesus is the title given to this work by our son, Jared Thomas Lathem. Jared also designed the cover. He is married to Lim and they have given us too perfect grandchildren, Zoe and Elijah. Jared is a pastor and in the opinion of his mom and dad, an excellent preacher. We are so proud of the man of God he has become. I get to read his sermons each week and wish I could have written them.

The first chapter in **The Acts of Jesus** is about friendship. I have been blessed with so many friends. Some of us began our friendship while we were still in diapers. Ironically, the older I get,

I think we may end our friendships in the same condition! I am thankful for life-long friends like Barry and Steve and Garry and so many others. I am thankful for deep and abiding friendships that have been developed along the way of ministry. Danny and James and Mike and David and Dan and David and John and Doug and Tom and Lindsey and… I am a blessed man. Too many friends to name here, to say nothing of the importance of the wives of those listed above.

One special friendship developed while I was in High School. It was the first year of use of the newly constructed Youth Building of Holbrook Campmeeting. Among the campers that first year was Gayle Hubbard. We became friends. We went to High School together. When I began preaching in 1972, Gayle would often accompany me and sing and work with the children and youth. When I finished Reinhardt College and moved to Wilmore, KY to attend Asbury College, Gayle was already there. I asked her to help me meet some girls. The first girl to whom she introduced me was Jane Baird, now my wife of 39 years and the love of my life.

When I transferred from Asbury Theological Seminary to Candler School of Theology I became friends with fellow student Rick Arnold. He served on my Professional Assessment Committee. After graduation he was appointed to a church in the same district in which I was appointed. Rick was the love of Gayle's life and they were married and became the first clergy couple to serve under appointment in the North Georgia Conference. Tragically, Rick died at far too young an age. But it was not before he had a tremendous impact on so many people, most of all, Gayle.

When the writing of **The Acts of Jesus** was finished, I needed an editor. Gayle volunteered. However, now she is Dr. Gayle Hubbard Arnold. Gayle has been a pioneer in so many ways for women in ministry. And now, even though disabled, continues to impact lives for Christ. Jane and I simply love Gayle. We are so grateful for her friendship. And we are grateful for the countless hours she has invested in editing this book. She is so very gracious.

Here is what Gayle had to say after editing and reading this manuscript several times:

"If your heart yearns for a deeper relationship with Christ, **The Acts of Jesus** *will allow you - chapter by chapter - to sit at the feet of Jesus and drink in the power of his never ending grace. Wherever you are in that walk, you will be renewed, refreshed, and revived!*

"Dr. Lathem's ministry has been marked by his gift of simply telling the truth about God's gift of grace through Jesus and seeing lives transformed . As you open each chapter of **The Acts of Jesus** *you will find yourself sitting at the feet of Jesus learning how you can more powerfully live as His disciple."*

Gayle, I am thankful for the over forty years we have been friends. I thank you for your tireless efforts in editing this work and in wrestling with your computer and in trying to teach me how to format a Word document. You were successful with the first two, but failed miserably with the third. However, the problem is not with the teacher!

Additionally, I must thank the great preachers who have helped shape my preaching: Reverends John Ozley, Clark McPherson, Claude Smithmier, Charles Shaw, Gene Winfrey, Billy Hardeman, Charles Cochran, Dennis Kinlaw, Ford Philpot, Dan Dunn, James Mooneyhan, Billy Graham, and, in print: John Wesley, Wallace Hamilton, Clovis Chappel, E. Stanley Jones and others.

Now, at this stage of my life, I have the great privilege of teaching preachers. This has been a part of my ministry for over 30 years, beginning with that first Teaching Parish group I supervised in

1981. It continues almost fulltime in Venezuela through the Seminario Wesleyano de Venezuela. The Seminary was established 10 years ago in partnership with Dan and Nancy Dunn and David and Carol Cosby. As I write this, I am sitting in our mission house in Venezuela and Dan and Nancy are here as well as David. Unfortunately for us, Carol had responsibilities in their work in Mexico City that prevented her from being here with us.

These friends have worked with me in the establishment of the most significant ministry of my life. I now get to teach preachers n Venezuela and have a small part in what God is doing to reach this nation for Christ. And new friendships have formed: Carlos and Wilmer and Alberto and Sam and Luis and Alex and Jesus, and Josue, and Alejandro and Yoe and Thoby and Juvenal and Franklin and so many others – as well as their gifted and gracious wives, most of whom are also in the seminary and serve in ministry in very significant ways. These are friendships I could never have imagined back when Gayle and I were in the Youth Building in the 1960's.

Friend, I hope you are helped in your journey of following Christ through the reading of **The Acts of Jesus**. I hope you will be a friend to someone who desperately needs your friendship. Perhaps you could give them a copy of this book and then see what God can do. If Jesus can turn water into wine, he can certainly take my feeble attempts at writing and turn them into means of transformation, hope, comfort and salvation.

Friend, thank you for giving a part of your life to reading **The Acts of Jesus.** May God richly bless you and may Jesus Christ be glorified through this work!

Rev. Dr. Warren Lathem

Dr. Warren Lathem is the President of the Wesleyan Seminary of Venezuela which he co-founded in 2002. He is the former District Superintendent of the Atlanta-Marietta District of the North Georgia Conference of the United Methodist Church. He has pastored churches since 1972.

His experience includes numerous seminars, training events, church consultations, mentoring, teaching in seminaries, crusade evangelism, ministry pioneer, camp meetings, and revivals on a national and international basis.

His last pastoral appointment was to the Mount Pisgah UM Church which he served for over 17 years. During his tenure, it grew to be the fourth largest UMC (based on average attendance) in the U.S. More importantly, during those years over 60% of the 5000 new members (net) who joined were by Profession of Faith.

He has always been committed to reaching the unchurched with the Good News of Jesus Christ. This led him to start many innovative ministries, e.g., Lay Missionary Training, The Journey, Recreation Ministry, Beacon of Hope Women's, The Summit Counseling Center and the first AID's ministry outside the perimeter of Atlanta. He began an After School Program, a Pre-school, an Elementary school, Middle school, and High school, enrolling over 900 children.

He co-founded the Aslan Group, a national church consulting firm. He also started what became the largest Hispanic ministry in the North Georgia Conference. In his last year as Senior minister, Mt Pisgah led the Conference in net new members. Thus, his ministry has been marked by transformed lives.

He has always been committed to the ministry of the laity and has partnered with the laity in most effective ways. His education includes an Associate in Arts; Reinhardt University; Bachelor of Arts, Asbury University; Masters of Divinity, Candler School of Theology, Emory University; Doctor of Ministry, McCormick Theological Seminary, University of Chicago.

He has served as Adjunct Faculty at Emory University, SIMBIMEX Theological Seminary of Mexico City as well as Professor at the Seminario Wesleyano de Venezuela.

Among his other published works are **Our Father...I Believe, Transformational Worship** (also available in Spanish), **A Prayer Campaign, Head 'Em Off At The Pass**, available at Lulu.com. **Preaching for a Response** (also available in Spanish), co-authored with Dr. Dan W. Dunn, is available at Bristol House (bristolhouseltd.com). All are available from the author along with other original works. Scripture quotes are from the New International Version unless otherwise noted.

Chapters

Chapter 1

Jesus Promised To Be Our Friend
John 15:15-16

John 15:15 I no longer call you servants, because a servant does not know his master's business. Instead, I have called you friends, for everything that I learned from my Father I have made known to you. 16 You did not choose me, but I chose you and appointed you to go and bear fruit--fruit that will last. Then the Father will give you whatever you ask in my name.

*****

Mark Twain said, "The holy passion of friendship is of so sweet and steady and loyal and enduring a nature that it will last through a whole lifetime if not asked to lend money!"

A Middle School English teacher asked her class to write imaginative definitions of a friend. One student said, "A friend is a pair of open arms in a society of arm-less people." Another said, "A friend is a warm bedroll on a cold and frosty night." "A friend is a mug of hot coffee on a damp, cloudy day." "A friend is a beautiful orchard in the middle of the desert." "A friend is a hot bath after you have walked 20 miles on a dusty road."(1) Lovely thoughts. Friendship... Friendship is clearly a wonderful thing.

However it is a rare thing. Recently, The Clergy Journal(2) shared disturbing information about making friends: 60% of men over 30 cannot identify a single person they would call a close friend. Of the 40% who list friends, most were made during childhood or school years. Most women can identify 5 or 6 women whom they call close friends. A closer look shows that a lot of these were functional relationships, but not necessarily deeply relational. Friendship is not easy to develop.

The Scripture Lesson is about friendship. If it has never occurred to you before, note that Christians were called "friends" before they were called Christians. That's right. The New Testament says, "it was in Antioch that the disciples were first called 'Christians'" -- long after the death of Jesus and the dispersion of his disciples in the early days of the church. But Jesus himself said to the disciples, "I have called you friends." Think about that. Let it sink in. "I have called you friends." Before anything else, "I have called you friends."

What are some of the characteristics of a good friendship?

1. Friends care about each other's welfare. That makes sense. If you are my friend, I want the best for you. I want people to think well of you. I want no harm to come to you.

2. Deep friendships are often forged in the midst of common suffering. Soldiers returning from the battlefield will always speak angrily of the ugliness of war and yet, in the same breath, they will talk with warmth about the friends that they made. I can guarantee you that as you and I are sitting here, deep friendships are being formed in the places where natural disasters occur; tornados and hurricanes and earthquakes and wildfires. People, who were initially perfect strangers, having passed together through a terrible storm, an earthquake, or some other natural disaster, will suddenly feel themselves to be the closest of friends and years later will sit and reminisce about their shared experiences.

3. Deep friendships are marked by sharing; even money, despite Mark Twain's humorous caveat. And more importantly, friends share what is inside. C. S. Lewis says, "Friendship is born

at that moment when one person says to another, 'What! You, too? I thought I was the only one."(3)

Years ago, I recall hearing of an old African-American woman who had spent some seventy years as servant to a southern belle from childhood into her dotage. Now the mistress had died, and in an effort to comfort this old black maid, a neighbor said, "I'm so sorry to hear of Aunt Lucy's death. You must miss her greatly. I know you were dear, dear friends."

"Yes'm," said the servant, "I am sorry she died. But we wasn't friends."

"Not friends," said the lady, "I know you were. I've seen you laughing and talking together lots of times."

"Yes'm, that's so," came the reply. "We've laughed together, and we've talked together, but we was just 'quaintances. You see, Miss Ruth, we ain't never shed no tears. Folks got to cry together before they is friends."(4)

There is a great difference between servanthood and friendship. One, however, is not mutually exclusive of the other. Have you ever had a boss with whom you were close friends? If so, you know it is possible to be both a servant and a close, intimate friend.

We are servants of Christ. That much is a given. He has chosen us to be his servants. But, and this is the good news, while we are servants, he treats us like friends.

Listen to his words again:
"I no longer call you servants, because a servant does not know his master's business. Instead, I have called you friends, for everything that I learned from my Father I have made known to you."

How is it we get to be Jesus' friend?

It begins with a choice - not our choice, but Jesus' own choice: "You did not choose me, but I chose you." That is called grace. Grace is unmerited favor, unmerited choice, unmerited love.

Let's begin with this thing of merit.

Do you merit the friendship of Jesus? Remember he is fully God and fully human. As fully God, he is sinless. He demands righteousness, blamelessness, and purity. His holiness requires holiness in us.

Are you righteous? Are you blameless? Are you pure? Ever fudged on an expense report? Ever taken a box of pens from the office? Ever cheated on a test? Ever told a lie? Ever acted selfishly? Ever been unfaithful? Ever exaggerated a story? Ever gossiped about someone? Ever committed adultery? Ever lusted? Ever coveted? Ever been prejudiced against someone because of their race, their religion, their social status, their gender, their age, their background?

A friend of mine told about going to a family reunion and proceeding to tell several jokes about trailer trash. She said everything got very quiet. Then she realized several of her cousins lived in trailers. It was a very awkward moment.

Humor at the expense of another may seem amusing, but reality may actually reach much deeper.

One of the finest people I have ever known lived in a mobile home. Dan Philpot ran the service station in Wilmore, KY when Jane and I were in school there. Dan was a natural evangelist. Uneducated and unpolished from the hills of eastern KY, he had a heart for

God and a heart for people. I went to more than one prayer-meeting in the service bay of Dan's station.

One of the reasons Dan lived in a trailer was because he was so generous. He helped many, many students at Asbury College and Seminary. They went on to serve as doctors and lawyers and missionaries and teachers and preachers all over the world. They were helped in getting their education by that kind, uneducated, humble man.

I am one of them. My car broke down. Major problems. The motor blew up. I had no money and no car. Yet I was the pastor of a country church. Dan learned of my problem and called me to come to his station. I got there and he handed me the keys to his personal car. He told me to drive it until I could get a new car or get mine fixed.

I could never feel superior to that so-called "trailer trash."

But haven't we all sinned at least in the area of prejudice? That, along with many other sins and our own sinful nature makes us unrighteous. We do not merit the friendship of the Righteous Son of God. We do not merit to be chosen by the Holy One of Israel.

Yet, He has chosen us anyway. Unmerited favor. Unmerited choice. Unmerited love. Unmerited.

But this grace is not just about the lack of merit on our part. No, it is much more than that. It is about a love that gives itself on our behalf.

Friendship often requires sacrifice of some sort, and, in some rare cases, even the supreme sacrifice. "Greater love has no one than this: to lay down one's life for one's friends," (John 15:13).

During the Vietnam War, a rural village had been bombarded with mortar shells and some shells landed on an orphanage run by missionaries. The missionaries and a few children were killed. Several other children were wounded, including an 8-year-old girl who had multiple injuries and was bleeding profusely.

A runner was sent to a near-by town to bring back a young Navy doctor and nurse who came with only their medical kits. The young girl was in critical condition and in need of an immediate blood transfusion. Blood typing indicated that neither American had the right blood. However, several of the uninjured children did.

The Navy doctor spoke some pidgin Vietnamese and the nurse some high school French. The children spoke no English, but some French. Using what language they had and sign language, they tried to explain to the frightened children that unless they could replace some of the girl's blood, she was going to die. They asked if anyone would be willing to give blood to help. Wide-eyed silence met their request. After several moments of eye-searching, a little hand went slowly up, dropped down, then went up again.

"Oh, thank you!" exclaimed the nurse in French, "What is your name?"

"Heng," came the reply.

Heng was quickly laid on a pallet; his arm swabbed with alcohol, the needle carefully inserted in his vein. After a moment he shuddered, covering his face with his free hand.

"Is it hurting, Heng?" asked the doctor. Heng shook his head no, but he kept sobbing, his eyes tightly closed, his fist in his mouth to stifle his sobs. Something was very wrong.

Just then a Vietnamese nurse arrived to help. Seeing Heng's distress, she spoke to him in Vietnamese, listened to him, quickly answered him, stroking his forehead, soothing and reassuring him. After a few moments, Heng stopped crying, opened his eyes, and a look of relief spread over his face. Looking up, the Vietnamese nurse explained to the Americans, "Heng thought he was dying. He misunderstood you. He thought you asked him to give all his blood to save the little girl."

"But why should he be willing to do that?" asked the Navy nurse.

The Vietnamese nurse repeated the question to Heng, who answered simply, "Because she is my friend."(5)

Have you ever had a friend like that? You may think you have no friend like Heng willing to die for you. However, you have at least one Friend like that. It was on a hill called Calvary, outside the city wall, and overlooking the town dump. It was there that your friend and my friend died that we might live. "No one has greater love than this, to lay down one's life for one's friends."

It is important to note we do not come upon this relationship with Jesus by accident. As Jesus reminded the twelve in that Upper Room, "You did not choose me but I chose you," (John 15:16).

You have been chosen. Jesus wants to be your friend. He has chosen to befriend you. Jesus has initiated the relationship.

Do you need a friend? He is the friend that sticks closer than a brother. *What a Friend We Have In Jesus*! states the old hymn:
> What a friend we have in Jesus,
> All our sins and griefs to bear,
> What a privilege to carry,
> Everything to God in prayer.
> Oh, what peace we often forfeit,

Oh, what needless pain we bear,
All because we do not carry,
Everything to God in prayer…
In His arms He'll take and shield you,
You will find a solace there."

I know some of you today need a friend who will go with you
through the valley of the shadow of death. Some of you need a
friend who won't betray you. Some of you need a friend who will
speak words of comfort and hope. Some of you need a friend to
help carry a very heavy burden. Some of you need a friend to
chase away your fears. Some of you need a friend to soothe your
troubled soul. Some of you need a friend to take away your guilt.
Some of you need a friend to give you a lasting security. Some of
you need a friend to help you raise your kids. Some of you need a
friend to help you work on your marriage.

Do you need a friend? Remember, Jesus said, "You are my
friends…You did not choose me, but I chose you."

I want to invite you to ask this Friend to come into your home,
your heart, your job, your fear, your marriage, your guilt, your
soul, your job, your life. He will. He has already chosen you by
his matchless grace, his unmerited favor. All you need to do is
invite him into your life. This Friend wants to be your friend.

Have you seen the bumper sticker with the slogan decrying drunk
driving, ""Friends Don't Let Friends Drive Drunk." A paraphrase
bumper sticker says, "Friends don't let friends die without Jesus." I
understand the sentiment, but I want to change it to "Friends don't
let friends LIVE without Jesus." Over and over and over let it be
said, Jesus is more than fire insurance. Jesus is joy. Jesus is peace.
Jesus is life abundant. Jesus is your friend.

*****

1. John Killinger, "A Celebration of Friendship," via Internet, Lectionary Homiletics
2. May/June 96. Quoted by Larry Linville, via Ecunet, "Sermonshop 1997 05 04," #4, 4/28/973. Fr. Charles Allen, S.J., via Internet, "Friendship," http://www/spirituality.org
4. A post by Susan Andrews, via PresbyNet, "Sermonshop 1997 05 04," #53, 5/1/97, brought this story to mind.
5. Carol Myers, Holland MI, via PresbyNet, "Bottom Drawer," #2717, 3/31/96
6. Thanks to Rev. Dr. David E. Leininger (The St. Paul Pulpit) for some information contained in this sermon.
7. "What A Friend We Have In Jesus," Joseph Scriven, 1855, Public Domain.

Chapter 2

Jesus Healed the Broken Spirit
John 4:1-26

John 4:1 The Pharisees heard that Jesus was gaining and baptizing more disciples than John, 2 although in fact it was not Jesus who baptized, but his disciples. 3 When the Lord learned of this, he left Judea and went back once more to Galilee. 4 Now he had to go through Samaria. 5 So he came to a town in Samaria called Sychar, near the plot of ground Jacob had given to his son Joseph. 6 Jacob's well was there, and Jesus, tired as he was from the journey, sat down by the well. It was about the sixth hour. 7 When a Samaritan woman came to draw water, Jesus said to her, "Will you give me a drink?" 8 (His disciples had gone into the town to buy food.) 9 The Samaritan woman said to him, "You are a Jew and I am a Samaritan woman. How can you ask me for a drink?" (For Jews do not associate with Samaritans.) 10 Jesus answered her, "If you knew the gift of God and who it is that asks you for a drink, you would have asked him and he would have given you living water." 11 "Sir," the woman said, "you have nothing to draw with and the well is deep. Where can you get this living water? 12 Are you greater than our father Jacob, who gave us the well and drank from it himself, as did also his sons and his flocks and herds?" 13 Jesus answered, "Everyone who drinks this water will be thirsty again, 14 but whoever drinks the water I give him will never thirst. Indeed, the water I give him will become in him a spring of water welling up to eternal life." 15 The woman said to him, "Sir, give me this water so that I won't get thirsty and have to keep coming here to draw water." 16 He told her, "Go, call your husband and come back." 17 "I have no husband," she replied. Jesus said to her, "You are right when you say you have no husband. 18 The fact is, you have had five husbands, and the man you now have is not your husband. What you have just said is

quite true." 19 "Sir," the woman said, "I can see that you are a
prophet. 20 Our fathers worshiped on this mountain, but you Jews
claim that the place where we must worship is in Jerusalem." 21
Jesus declared, "Believe me, woman, a time is coming when you
will worship the Father neither on this mountain nor in Jerusalem.
22 You Samaritans worship what you do not know; we worship
what we do know, for salvation is from the Jews. 23 Yet a time is
coming and has now come when the true worshipers will worship
the Father in spirit and truth, for they are the kind of worshipers the
Father seeks. 24 God is spirit, and his worshipers must worship in
spirit and in truth." 25 The woman said, "I know that Messiah"
(called Christ) "is coming. When he comes, he will explain
everything to us." 26 Then Jesus declared, "I who speak to you
am he."

*****

One of our favorite places on earth is the high desert of Venezuela
at the Lugar Altissimo United Methodist Church. We have spent
many significant times there and our younger son was married in
this church built and dedicated in memory of his brother. We love
the place and the people. Some of our friends have been there and
love them as well.

But one thing we do not love about the place is how very dry it is.
It is so arid the liquid is just sucked out of your body. During the
day it is hot and dry and if you are not very careful you can
become extremely dehydrated very quickly – and I can tell you
from experience, that is no fun.

I remember another time I found myself in a very dry, hot and
inhospitable place. It was at the location of today's Scripture
Lesson – Jacob's well. I was taking a tour of the Holy Land. The
bus stopped at a little fork in the road and we got out. Was it ever
hot, in the middle of November! And it was so dry! We went into
the little Orthodox church that had been built over the site of

Jacob's well. I dropped the bucket into the well and drew up some cool, refreshing water and passed it around to those in our group.

Then I remembered the story John told in the fourth chapter of his Gospel. Jesus was traveling from northern Israel back to the south, to Jerusalem. He went through Samaria, or the West Bank as we call it today. He did not travel in an air-conditioned Mercedes bus like I did. He walked. Every single step stirred up dust and the arid atmosphere sucked the moisture out of his body.

By noon he was tired and hungry. He stopped at Jacob's Well. He sat down to rest and sent his disciples into the little village of Sychar to buy some lunch.

As he sat there, a woman approached. She came to the well to draw water for her needs and the needs of her household. As she approached the well, Jesus asked her for a drink of water. This was the beginning of a most interesting conversation.

First, she was amazed that he would speak to her. Why was that? It was hot and he didn't have a rope or bucket to use to get any water. She did and she was there to get water out of the well. Why was she surprised that he would ask her for a drink.

There are several reasons, the first ones dealing with who he was. He was a Jew. She was a Samaritan. The Jews would have nothing to do with Samaritans. They saw them as a mongrel race. They were of a mixed ethnic background. They had an inferior heritage and an inferior religion, as far as the Jews were concerned. So the Jews avoided the Samaritans.

She was also surprised by this conversation because he was a man. Jewish men did not speak to a woman in public unless she was accompanied by her husband. It was a man's world in which women had no voice or vote. Men ruled. A man would not stoop to converse with something or someone so lowly as a woman.

One of the great hurdles to overcome in our relations with Arab countries today is the fact that the Secretary of State is a woman. Hillary Clinton is a capable woman. However, conservative Arabs will not even speak to a woman and think of a woman as a possession, certainly not an equal. He was a Jewish man living in a culture that embraced similar prejudices concerning women.

She was further surprised by the conversation because he asked her for a drink of water. Our Scripture lesson in verse 9 shows her surprise: "How can you ask me for a drink?" John then inserts for our understanding the parenthetical statement "For the Jews do not associate with the Samaritans." A more accurate translation might be that Jews do not eat or drink with Samaritans. Or even more precisely, the Jews do not use utensils used by the Samaritans. Here was a Jew asking for a drink from her water jar.

She was even more surprised by the conversation because he was obviously a Rabbi, or Teacher. Women were not allowed to be taught to read. No rabbi would stoop to converse with a woman regarding spiritual or religious things. They were ignorant, as far as the rabbi was concerned.

But her greatest surprise came when this male Jewish rabbi who was thirstily resting on the well curb said to her, "If you knew the gift of God and who it is that asks for you for a drink, you would have asked him and he would have given you living water."

What kind of craziness is that? He had no bucket or rope. Was he greater than Jacob who dug the well? Could he give her water that would satisfy so completely that she would not have to keep coming to the well every day – in the desert? She was surprised by what he said and the fact that he said anything at all to her.

She was not only surprised because of who he was. She was surprised because of who she was. Yes, she was of mongrel heritage, and yes, she was just a woman, but there was more.

She had a failed marriage. The only status a woman could have in her culture was that afforded by a marriage. Her first marriage had ended. We don't know how or why, but it was over. Not only had her first marriage ended but so had the 2nd and the 3rd and the 4th and the 5th. Five failed relationships. Five failed marriages. Five times a failure.

But it gets worse. She seems to have given up on marriage, or men had given up on her. When she meets Jesus she is not only marked by her failed marriages, she is now seeing some man, sleeping with him and he is not her husband. Was he married? Probably. So she now is the "other woman." The "Home-breaker." The "Whore of the village."

Her life had gotten so bad she refused to be around the other women of her village. They came to draw water early in the morning when it was cool and at night after the sun set. There they would talk and socialize, like at a small town post office. Guess what one of the things they talked about was. Her. That is right. When they got together she was the topic of their conversation. She was the object of their ridicule, their hate, their spite. So she only went to the well when no one else would be there.

And here sat Jesus, speaking to a Samaritan woman who experienced five failed marriages and was living an immoral life. Whether it was because of circumstances or her own proclivities, or both, we just don't know.

Now in John's Gospel, words often have double meanings. For instance, when Jesus said he was the Bread of Life, he did not mean literal bread. Of course people misunderstood him. They wanted bread, regular bread. They wanted an easy life, a problem-free life, one in which they were free from the daily toil for something to eat. But Jesus was not speaking about ordinary bread. He was using it as a teaching tool for a much greater truth. He was saying he was the answer to the hunger in the soul of humanity – a hunger that nothing else could satisfy.

Here when Jesus spoke about living water, he was not speaking about H2O, he was using it as a metaphor for something much greater. He was speaking of a water that could satisfy the thirst of her life, not just quench the thirst of her body.

So what did Jesus do? He said to her, "ask him and he will give you living water." What was he doing? What was he talking about? What did he do?

1. He talked to her. No one else cared. After five broken marriages, and an adulterous life it appeared as if no one would ever care for her. People were only interested in her for what they could get from her. No one cared for her. But Jesus did. This is the longest recorded conversation of Jesus in all the Gospels. It is the conversation between a Jewish rabbi and a woman of ill-repute.

2. He asked for her help. No one else would. No one else would ask for her help. She had nothing to offer to the prim and proper world of her village. She had no value. She had no worth. She was to be ostracized, gossiped about, shunned, and ridiculed. She was nothing. But Jesus saw beyond the circumstances of her life and saw a woman whose spirit was broken. So he asked her for help. Why? Because he wanted to establish a relationship with her. No one else would.

3. He gave to her. No one else did. Everyone else took from her until there was nothing left to take. All that was left of her life was a dried up husk. Dry and dusty. Empty and shriveled. Jesus offered to fill her life with living water. It was something that would satisfy the thirst of her soul. It was something that would fill the emptiness of her life. It was something that would quench the fire of remorse and regret. It was Living Water.

Just what was this Living Water Jesus offered to her? How could she get it? She obviously didn't understand. That's why she said, "Sir, you have nothing to draw with and the well is deep. Where can you get this living water?"

Then followed a long theological discussion culminating in her confession that one day a Messiah would come. Jesus revealed the Messiah and the source for the Living Water when he then said, "I … am he."

Jesus revealed that he was the answer to the question of her life. He was the water for the thirst of her life. He was the source for the meaning of her life. He was the healing for the brokenness of her life.

Jesus could and would and did heal her broken spirit. We didn't read the rest of the story, but after Jesus gave her this Living Water she ran back to town to tell the news. This woman who avoided contact with other women, who had experienced nothing but regrets at the hands of men, who was broken, dejected and alone, ran to the center of town to tell them what Jesus had done for her.

Let me ask you: Is your spirit broken? Have you been riding a merry-go-round of new relationships, new jobs, new self-improvement schemes, new toys, new substances, new religions?

They are all trips to the well. They may satisfy for a little while, but soon you get thirsty again. The haunting emptiness returns.

Why? Because only Jesus can satisfy your soul. Only Jesus can heal what is broken in your life. Only Jesus can give you living water so you don't have to keep going back to the same old tired wells.

A broken spirit is the most difficult thing to heal. Only Jesus can heal the broken spirit.

Are you broken? Is your life reflected in the life of this woman? Maybe your brokenness is very visible to others, as was the case with this woman. Or maybe you are the only one to know about the brokenness in your life. Do you need healing for your broken heart, your broken spirit?

You have read the Samaritan woman's story. We offer healing in Jesus' name: Healing for whatever brokenness exists in your life.

We invite you to the healing only Jesus can give. This may be a very private thing, so we will deal with this in a very private way – just between you and God.

Let me simply remind you, this is not a secret formula, this is not some get-well quick scheme. What we have to offer is Jesus.

If you are aware of your need for healing some brokenness in your life I invite you to pray this prayer for healing:

Lord Jesus, I need your healing.
You know what is on my heart.
You know where I am broken.
In your Name, I ask you to heal me.
Take away the hurt and pain.

Take away the resentment and anger.
Take away the fear and doubt.
In their place, fill my heart with your presence.
Fill my heart with your Spirit.
Fill my heart with your forgiveness.
Fill my heart with your love.
Thank you, Jesus. AMEN

Chapter 3

Jesus Promised To Be Our Way
John 14:1-7

John 14:1 "Do not let your hearts be troubled. Trust in God; trust
also in me. 2 In my Father's house are many rooms; if it were not
so, I would have told you. I am going there to prepare a place for
you. 3 And if I go and prepare a place for you, I will come back
and take you to be with me that you also may be where I am. 4
You know the way to the place where I am going." 5 Thomas said
to him, "Lord, we don't know where you are going, so how can we
know the way?" 6 Jesus answered, "I am the way and the truth
and the life. No one comes to the Father except through me. 7 If
you really knew me, you would know my Father as well. From
now on, you do know him and have seen him."

*****

Several years ago our church was doing a mission project in
Jamaica, about two hours west of Kingston. The staff person who
was scheduled to go on the trip had to cancel at the last minute. So
I was drafted to go down a couple of days ahead of the rest of the
team and make the final preparations. I had to fly into Montego
Bay because we were also taking several items to the infirmary in
St. Anne's Bay where we had sent several mission teams. So after
dropping off those supplies, I made the long drive in my little
rental car across the island. When I got near Kingston, I was
unsure which way to go. At a major intersection, a crowd of
people were gathered waiting on a ride home from work. I stopped
to ask directions. Immediately two women hopped into the back-
seat and sat down. They introduced themselves. One was a school
teacher in Kingston and the other was a government worker.
When I explained my need for directions to Lioneltown, they said

that was where they were going and would be glad to show me the way. So I started off with my two new friends in the back-seat.

On the way there I explained that I needed to meet with the pastor, Freddy, and then get back to Kingston to meet another team member who was flying in about ten o'clock that night. They were both obviously alarmed and told me emphatically that I could not be in Kingston after dark. I tried to dismiss their fears for me, telling them I had been all over Jamaica and had never feared for my safety. However they kept insisting, "You cannot be in Kingston after dark.

When we got to our destination, I let them out and drove to the manse, the pastor's house. He was not there so I had to wait a few minutes. Upon his arrival, we greeted each other warmly. Then he asked about my schedule for the rest of the day. I told him I had to be at the Kingston Airport about 10:30 to pick up a member of the church. He looked at his watch and said, "You have to leave now!" I said, "Oh, I've got plenty of time. It's only a couple of hours away." But he insisted I leave, started ushering me to the car, and said those ominous words, "You can't be in Kingston after dark!" No protesting on my part would convince him as he closed the door and sent me away.

By the time I got to Kingston it was dark. All I could hear were the words of both women and the pastor, "You can't be in Kingston after dark." As I drove into that teeming city, the streets were filled with people. I had to ease the car through the mass of bodies, blowing the horn and driving 5 or 10 miles an hour. People were literally surrounding the car. About that time I realized I was totally lost. I did not know where I was nor how to get to the airport. I had a map, but there were no road signs and no way to determine my location to find a starting point on the map.

Then it turned ugly. People started hitting on the car, yelling obscenities, and making threatening gestures. I was scared. I felt like I had a flashing neon sign on top of the car reading, "Stupid rich American white man in Kingston after dark. Come and get it!"

So I started driving a little faster, now using the car to part the mass of people, knocking a few out of the way in the process. I was making better time, but had no idea where I was or where I was going.

Then straight in front of me I saw a service station. However, there must have been over 100 men gathered in and around the station, standing around enjoying the cooler Jamaican evening. I had no choice, I had to pull into the station and ask directions. As I pulled to a stop, the owner sprinted out to the car, told me how to get to the airport and urged me to be on my way.

As I pulled away from the station, I noticed something I had not seen before. The sign above the station was lit and each letter of the name was lit independently, spelling out the name of the company, "SHELL." Only on this night on the sign, one letter was not lit. The sign simply spelled, "_HELL."

I had felt like that was where I was until the station manager told me the way.

It was the night before his own death. Jesus was spending his last precious hours on earth with his closest friends. They were frightened. They knew the danger he was in, and by association with him, the danger they faced. Locked in an unidentified "upper room," they considered their plight. Did death await Jesus the next day? Did death await them all? Jesus had already been warned, "You can't be in Jerusalem after dark." But he had come anyway and they reluctantly followed.

Now they were afraid. Jesus sensed their anxiety. So he spoke words of comfort to them: 14:1 "Do not let your hearts be troubled. Trust in God; trust also in me. 2 In my Father's house are many rooms; if it were not so, I would have told you. I am going there to prepare a place for you. 3 And if I go and prepare a place for you, I will come back and take you to be with me that you also may be where I am. 4 You know the way to the place where I am going."

In response to those wonderful words, Thomas, "Doubting Thomas" we call him, blurted out what was on the minds of all of them there, 5 Thomas said to him, "Lord, we don't know where you are going, so how can we know the way?"

Then Jesus issued this great "I AM" statement. It is one of the seven great "I AM" statements in the gospel of John.

1. "I am the BREAD OF LIFE,"
2. "I am the LIGHT OF THE WORLD,"
3. "I am the DOOR,"
4. "I am the GOOD SHEPHERD,"
5. "I am the RESURRECTION AND THE LIFE,"
6. "I am the TRUE VINE,"
7. "I am the WAY, the TRUTH, and the LIFE."

"I am the way, the truth and the life." What does that mean? What did it mean to them and what does it mean to us?

When Jesus said to his disciples "I AM THE WAY," he was saying, "I AM THE WAY" to God. He does not merely show the way by example, He is not merely a prophet to teach the way, nor does He merely guide in the way by strong assistance. HE IS HIMSELF THE WAY!

When he said "I AM THE TRUTH," he is not only the true God and true man, but HE IS TRUTH ITSELF! He is the sum and substance of all the truth of the gospel, of all the promises, of all the light and shadows; and he is the true way in opposition to every false way. Pilate asked, "What is truth?" Our Lord answers that question here in John 14, "I AM THE TRUTH."

When he said, "I AM THE LIFE," he speaks of life as opposed to death--all death and all kinds of death. He has life in Himself. He is the source and giver of life. He is the light of life, the word of life, and He came that we might have life. "He that hath the Son of God hath life; and he that hath not the Son of God hath not life" (I John 5:12).

What does all this have to do with you and me?

- I need and want to know the way.
- I need and want to know the truth.
- I need and want to experience LIFE with a capital "L."
- I need and want to know how to connect with God.

1. I need and want to know the way.

When I was recently in Venezuela, Dan Dunn and I were driving the hour and a half from the Seminary to Nirgua where we would be teaching a Seminary extension course. About half way there we missed a turn. The highway was a divided highway with no place to turn around. So for 6 or 7 miles he drove while I studied a map to see if we could take another route. It was getting close to dark and the only alternative was a small road though the mountains. Which way to go? We finally decided to drive until we found a place to turn around and go back to the way we knew.

That is so much like life as we know it. There are so many ways open to us. Is it the way of education? Career? Family? Wealth? Recreation? Success? Self-indulgence? Creativity? Sacrifice? What is the WAY?

Jesus said, "I AM THE WAY!" While there are many ways open to you and me, any way other than the way of Jesus will lead us to being lost and disoriented in life. There is only one way. His name is Jesus. He is the way in life. He is the way in death. He is the way with our families. He is the way with our careers. He is the way with our education. He is the way, the only way, which leads to life

2. I need and want to know the TRUTH.

There are so many espousing truth. The Republicans have the truth. The Democrats have the truth. The Libertarians have the truth. The Independents have the truth. The rich have the truth. The poor have the truth. The liberal theologians have the truth. The conservative theologians have the truth. The fundamentalists have the truth. The educated have the truth. The uneducated have the truth. The establishment has the truth. The anti-establishment have the truth.

Where do you look to find the truth? The AJC? CNN? MSNBC? FoxNEWS? The Huffington Report? Neil? Rush? ABC? The Bible? The Bible certainly contains the truth. But Jesus IS the truth. Many things can be true. Only one is TRUTH! His name is Jesus.

You may know the rule of 72 is true. You may know 5280 feet is the true distance of a mile. You may know the true balance in your retirement account. You might even know what is true in the assassination of John F. Kennedy. But if you do not know Jesus, you do not know TRUTH.

3. I need and want to experience LIFE with a capital "L."

I get things beautifully structured for myself. I hedge all my bets by careful, calculated living. Then some catastrophe hits, or more subtly things start leaking around the edges. My best plans for life can't guarantee the health and safety of the people I love. Haven't you found it to be the same? Those of us who are the most organized often end up the most frustrated because we can only organize a part of our lives. Our best-written scenarios don't turn out the way we'd always like.

You see, there is no way I can hedge my bet, guaranteeing for my loved ones or for myself the kind of life I would plan. At the moment I least expect it, the ball takes a crazy bounce. My best plans are no guarantee of my own existence here.

Jesus said, "I am the life." He is the absolute embodiment of life with a capital "L".

You see, His life puts purpose behind the inexplicable. I can't make any sense of a child being abducted, raped and murdered. I can't make any sense of a beautiful mother being killed by a drunken driver. I can't make any sense of a plane filled with people falling from the sky. I can't make any sense out of malignant cells stripping life from the people I love.

But Jesus sees the overall pattern. He didn't create evil. He doesn't like disease. But He has a way of taking the worst tragedies and enabling us to survive, and to be more than survivors. We can trust Him with the lives of our loved-ones. We can trust Him with our own lives because He has made provision for us.

His life turns our insignificance into significance. Jesus says that you have worth, that you are not an accident. The greatest of difficulties need not conquer you. He gives you His creative energy to handle whatever comes your way.

His life equips you for life beyond this human existence.

That's what makes a funeral service for one who died in Christ a joyous occasion. Yes, there are tears for ourselves, those of us who remain. It's at this point the resurrection message impacts us in all of its creative promise. We realize life does not end with death. The Apostle Paul wrote: "For if the dead are not raised, then Christ has not been raised either. And if Christ has not been raised, your faith is futile; you are still in your sins. Then those also who have fallen asleep in Christ are lost. If only for this life we have hope in Christ, we are to be pitied more than all men. But Christ has indeed been raised from the dead, the firstfruits of those who have fallen asleep" (I Cor.15:16-21).

He has equipped us for eternity. He has prepared a place for us. He will take us to be with Himself. Life in heaven with Jesus is the perfect existence. This is the promise of God's Word.

I need and want to experience life with a capital "L". I have decided irrevocably to take Jesus at His word and believe that He is life. How about you? That's one ultimate you and I can commit ourselves to now!

4. I need and want to know how to connect with God.

The deepest longing of your soul and mine is to know God. As children we hungered to know God. We believed whatever we were told about the nature of God. Our hearts longed for a connection for God.

As we grew older, we stifled our hunger for God by reaching for other things. But the desire to be connected to God has never gone away. We are here today because we want to know God. We want to experience God. We want to be connected to God.

It is my calling to tell you how you can know, connect with, and experience God. The way is Jesus! Do you know him? Have you committed your life to him? Do you believe in him?

To know Jesus is to know God. "If you really knew me, you would know my Father as well," (John 8:19).

Today, I am aware there are people reading this book who do not know Jesus. You may have heard about him, sung to him, prayed to him, taught your children about him, but you do not know him. It is time to change that.

I want to invite you to receive Jesus as the WAY, the TRUTH, and the LIFE for you. It is not enough that your mother knew Jesus. You must make your own faith commitment to him. You must receive him as your own Lord and Savior.

Do you want to know the WAY? Do you want to know the TRUTH? Do you want to know the LIFE? Then come to Jesus. There is no other way. There is no other truth. There is no other life.

Do you want to know the Way?

Jesus is the way!

Chapter 4

Jesus Saw What Others Did Not See
Luke 7:36-50

Luke 7:36-50 Now one of the Pharisees invited Jesus to have dinner with him, so he went to the Pharisee's house and reclined at the table. 37 When a woman who had lived a sinful life in that town learned that Jesus was eating at the Pharisee's house, she brought an alabaster jar of perfume, 38 and as she stood behind him at his feet weeping, she began to wet his feet with her tears. Then she wiped them with her hair, kissed them and poured perfume on them. 39 When the Pharisee who had invited him saw this, he said to himself, "If this man were a prophet, he would know who is touching him and what kind of woman she is--that she is a sinner." 40 Jesus answered him, "Simon, I have something to tell you." "Tell me, teacher," he said. 41 "Two men owed money to a certain moneylender. One owed him five hundred denarii, and the other fifty. 42 Neither of them had the money to pay him back, so he canceled the debts of both. Now which of them will love him more?" 43 Simon replied, "I suppose the one who had the bigger debt canceled." "You have judged correctly," Jesus said. 44 Then he turned toward the woman and said to Simon, "Do you see this woman? I came into your house. You did not give me any water for my feet, but she wet my feet with her tears and wiped them with her hair. 45 You did not give me a kiss, but this woman, from the time I entered, has not stopped kissing my feet. 46 You did not put oil on my head, but she has poured perfume on my feet. 47 Therefore, I tell you, her many sins have been forgiven--for she loved much. But he who has been forgiven little loves little." 48 Then Jesus said to her, "Your sins are forgiven." 49 The other guests began to say among themselves, "Who is this who even forgives sins?" 50 Jesus said to the woman, "Your faith has saved you; go in peace."

*****

Someone has said, "There is no saint without a past and no sinner without a future." That certainly is illustrated in today's Scripture Lesson. Here we encounter a remarkable saint who has a most despicable past and a sinner with an untarnished future. Both the saint and the sinner are seen in the same person – the woman.

Jesus asked Simon the Pharisee, "Do you see this woman?" I want to ask you the same question: Do you see this woman?

Now when we read this scripture, we can see Jesus. Even though he is larger than life to us, we can still envision him.

We can see the Pharisee. We have all known some religious or political leader, wealthy and self-satisfied.

But can we see this woman? Oh, we can see a prostitute. We are used to seeing them on the streets of our cities, on many of our TV shows, interviewed on Talk Shows, portrayed in movie after movie, invading our homes over the internet through unsolicited email trash. Certainly, we recognize a prostitute when we see one, at least the portrayal of a Hollywood movie prostitute.

But can we see this woman? Not a prostitute. Not a woman of ill repute. Not a woman that the whole town knows, at least by reputation. Not a woman who has flaunted her immorality, rejected God's plan for her life, enticed others to participate in her sin, been the victim of the powerful lust of powerful people, sold her virtue to the highest bidder. Not that woman. That woman is not in this scene.

Look carefully. What do you see? A sinner? That is what the
Pharisee saw. He saw a sinner, a "hamartolos – Greek." Yet when
he called her a sinner, he did not mean what the Greek word meant
in its pure form. For it simply meant, "sinner." It is a word that
can and is used to describe all humankind. As Paul says, "For all
have sinned." We are all sinners.

When Simon the Pharisee called her a sinner, he was being much
more specific. He is identifying her as a prostitute. Was she a
prostitute? Probably. She was certainly known in the whole town
because of her immorality. Simon saw a sinner, a prostitute, an
unwelcome intruder, an unworthy person, a worthless individual,
spoiled goods.

What do you see?

First, however, we need to ask:

What did Jesus see? On the surface it is easy to note that

- Jesus saw a woman who washed his feet – with her tears;
- a woman who dried his feet with her hair;
- a woman who bathed his feet in her kisses;
- a woman who anointed his feet with expensive perfume.
- Oh, but Jesus saw much more than that.

Jesus saw a woman who was so overcome with gratitude and joy
that it erupted in an extravagant display of love and devotion.

Everyone else at the dinner saw a woman of ill repute slip into the
elegant home of a distinguished religious leader and proceed to
make a complete fool out of her immodest self and the visiting
preacher. They saw a prostitute who was not to be intimidated by

social customs or norms, openly flaunt her lack of social status and decorum.

They also saw a preacher who was so taken by the actions of this woman that he allowed her to behave in such an unseemly and embarrassing fashion. This Jesus must not be a prophet of any high regard or he would have perceived what kind of woman she was and made sure he had no contact with her. If he was any kind of admirable religious leader, he would have recognized her for what she was and gotten out of her grasp.

Several years ago, there were hardly any restaurants near the church I was serving. Finally a few began to open. One of the first was a sports bar just about a mile from the church. About once a week, I would have lunch there with a staff member or church member. I got to know the bartender since she would often wait on our table. She discovered what kind of coffee I liked and would make a point to put on a fresh pot when I came in the door.

I forgot to tell you that she was young, blond and absolutely beautiful. And, she didn't dress like she was on her way to Sunday School, either. Over time I discovered she had a rather troubled past. Yet she was trying to pull herself out of the hole created for her by an abusive father and some rather unscrupulous men.

She started coming to church. After several weeks she asked Jesus to come into her heart. Her life was changed in an instant! She discovered a forgiveness she could have never even imagined, a love that she had never known, a peace that was beyond understanding. She fell in love with Jesus.

She continued to work for a while in the sports bar as the daytime bartender. One day my wife and I went in there for lunch. All of a sudden, this beautiful, young, immodestly dressed, beautiful blond bounded from behind the bar and ran up to me and threw her arms around me and gave me a great big kiss on the cheek.

I saw a new-born Christian who was so over-joyed by her experience of grace that she could not hold it in, but wanted to thank me for the small part I had played in her coming to Christ.

That is not what Jane saw.... You can guess what Jane saw! I finally realized that what I was seeing and what Jane was seeing were two entirely different scenes. Then I quickly introduced the young lady to my wife and told her how she had just recently become a Christian.

The young lady took our beverage order and left. I still had some more explaining to do.

However, today I am reminded of just how differently I saw her from the way my wife saw her. Now there is not nearly enough in me that is like Jesus. However, at this one point, I think I understand what Jesus saw that day when he looked at that woman. He didn't see what the Pharisee saw. He didn't see what the rest of the crowd saw. He didn't see a shameful prostitute. He saw a woman who, though guilty of committing many sins, was forgiven and made new.

Jesus saw a woman who was so overwhelmed by grace that she couldn't hold it in. Jesus saw a woman who was so joyful she just had to show it. Jesus saw a woman who was so filled with gratitude she just had to express it.

No, Jesus did not see at all what the other folk at the dinner saw. He loved so unreservedly he simply saw a woman who had been made new by grace. He saw a woman whose checkered past was gone. A woman whose guilt simply did not exist anymore. A woman who was free to lead a new life unencumbered with the past.

Why did he see that instead of what the rest of them saw? Because of his great love for her and because of the transforming power of grace in her life. You see, this woman was a forgiven sinner. She had a fresh start, a new beginning.

Therefore, what she did was not strange to Jesus, not inappropriate to Jesus. He understood what she was doing and why.

What was she doing? Look at the story again. See the hair, the tears, the washing of the feet, the kisses, the ointment. Careful now. You may see it the same way Simon the Pharisee saw it. But that's not how Jesus saw what she was doing.

When he saw her kneel at his feet, he knew what was in her heart. She didn't care whose house it was, what was going on, or who saw her. She had found her Savior. She had found the one who had made her new. She had found the one who loved without measure. She had found the one who had lifted her out of the pit of sin that had been destroying her life. She had found Jesus. She would bow in absolute surrender at his feet.

When he saw her tears, he knew their meaning. Some people think of tears only as expressions of sorrow. I want to tell you, the most meaningful tears are tears of joy. Have you ever cried tears of joy? I have on many occasions. However, two of these stand out in my mind: when both our boys were born I cried tears of joy. If you have children and didn't cry tears of joy, there's something wrong with you.

She cried tears of joy because she had become a new person, she had experienced new life, it was as if she had been born again, for she had been. Her joy overflowed in her tears. Jesus saw them for what they were. Others observing might have thought the tears were tears of remorse or sorrow. Jesus saw them as the tears of joy they surely were.

When she began to bathe his feet with her tears, he knew why she was doing it. As she knelt at his feet and began to cry tears of joy, she noticed that he had suffered a great indignity. Upon arrival at Simon's house he had not received even the most basic hospitality. He had not received the most rudimentary respect. No one had washed his feet, as was the custom. She noted this lack of even ordinary respect shown to her Lord.

So her tears began to flow even more and she began to bathe his feet with her tears. Others may not have understood her act, but Jesus did.

When he saw her let down her hair, he knew what it was about. In her culture, a woman was not to be seen in public with her hair down. She put it up when she got married and no other man was to ever see it down except her husband. Here this woman of fame for her immodesty of the past confirms others' opinion of her by taking down her hair in the presence of a man. But Jesus knew it was not an act of immodesty but of love and gratitude as she began to dry his feet with the hair of her head. There was nothing unholy about what she was doing. It was a holy act of service she was rendering to her Savior.

When she began to kiss his feet, Jesus knew what she was doing. Kissing the feet of a person was a recognized sign of deep reverence, especially toward honored teachers. Here she was in the house of a Pharisee, a person of respect and authority, perhaps one who was accustomed to having someone kiss his feet. But she did not bow before Simon. She knelt before Jesus, washed his feet with her tears, dried them with her hair, and kissed his feet in complete surrender to his grace.

When she poured the perfume on his feet, Jesus knew what she was doing. Simon had not anointed the head of Jesus when he invited him into his home. Even though it was customary to do so, like the failure to wash his feet, it was just one more indignity Jesus suffered at the hand of the ungracious host.

She could not bear to see her Savior treated so poorly. She had a small alabaster bottle of perfume tied around her neck. Most women of her day did the same thing. The perfume created a very pleasant aroma. She opened her most valuable possession and poured the perfume on his feet in an outrageous expression of love and gratitude. Others may have thought she had lost her mind. She was doing the most sane thing of her life.

Jesus had loved her so unreservedly that she had to show her gratitude and love for her Savior. He had changed her life. Nothing was too extravagant for him. She owed him everything she had and more. To pour the costly perfume on his feet meant little to her. What was important to her was the expression of her gratitude, the response she gave to the one who had changed her life. In the economy of God, giving is always a response. We give because of what we have received. So she did.

We are not going to worry with Simon the Pharisee today. He'll have to wait for another time. We are going to relish the extravagant display of love of this woman for one who forgave her sin.

True Worship is extravagant.

Worship is viewed by others as foolish, even crazy.

Worship is not appreciated by those who do not engage in it.

Worship flows out of a heart of thanksgiving, gratitude and
    praise.

Worship flows from a humble heart.

Worship evokes giving.

Worship is a testimony.

Others may see our expressions of love and gratitude for Jesus as
outrageous and extravagant, but we know why we erupt with joy.
We know the Savior and we have experienced his redeeming love.
Praise his matchless Name. We know there is no saint without a
past and no sinner without a future. We believe the Gospel and its
power to save to the uttermost.

Has your experience of the grace of Jesus gotten deep enough into
your soul to produce this kind of unbridled, boundless, extravagant
worship? Have you ever been so overwhelmed by His grace, his
unmerited love and forgiveness, that you had to make a fool of
yourself for Jesus?

That is exactly what I am going to ask you to do today. I am going
to ask you to make a public profession of faith in Jesus Christ. I
want to invite you to him. Your life may appear to be in good
order, but you know in your heart lives deceit, and hopelessness,
hostility, doubt, fear, anxiety, sin. Maybe sin of adultery. Maybe
sin of idolatry. Maybe sin of theft. Maybe sin of lying. Whatever it
is you know in your heart that you need Jesus.

I want to invite you to do an extravagant thing today. I want to
invite you to come to the front here and tell the pastor, "I need
Jesus." That is all you have to say. Come and take your pastor by
the hand and just say, "I need Jesus." He will help you from there.

Are you a person with a past for which you are genuinely sorry?
Are you a person without hope or direction for the future?

Jesus offers life to you.

Chapter 5

Jesus Taught the Reality of Heaven
Matthew 5:1-12

5:1 Now when he saw the crowds, he went up on a mountainside and sat down. His disciples came to him, 2 and he began to teach them, saying: 3 "Blessed are the poor in spirit, for theirs is the kingdom of heaven. 4 Blessed are those who mourn, for they will be comforted. 5 Blessed are the meek, for they will inherit the earth. 6 Blessed are those who hunger and thirst for righteousness, for they will be filled. 7 Blessed are the merciful, for they will be shown mercy. 8 Blessed are the pure in heart, for they will see God. 9 Blessed are the peacemakers, for they will be called sons of God. 10 Blessed are those who are persecuted because of righteousness, for theirs is the kingdom of heaven. 11 "Blessed are you when people insult you, persecute you and falsely say all kinds of evil against you because of me. 12 Rejoice and be glad, because great is your reward in heaven, for in the same way they persecuted the prophets who were before you."

*****

A lot of folks are looking for heaven on earth. We try to create a life free of pain, disappointment, despair, hunger and longing. This is especially true of those of us who cling to the American Dream. We want to create a life of security, fulfillment, and plenty. One of the primary reasons is we want to build a hedge around our lives so as to avoid the suffering we see in the lives of others around us.

So we live in "heavenly" houses, drive "heavenly" cars, travel to "heavenly" vacation destinations, eat "heavenly" rich food and drink "heavenly" champagne. We dress in "heavenly" clothes, invest in "heavenly" stock options, work at "heavenly" jobs and work out to develop "heavenly" bodies.

Then something happens to shatter our "heaven on earth:"

- something like a break-in and the molestation of a little girl in our neighborhood;
- something like the disappearance of a young mother practically in our backyard;
- something like the bombing of a church in Nigeria;
- something like the loss of a job;
- something like the incarceration of a child;
- something like the death of a spouse, just to name a few.

For some of us, life had been mostly idyllic. The worst we have had to deal with is teenage acne, until now. We had led a charmed life, free of significant suffering or pain. Wonderful parents. Great social life. Good grades. Great job. Beautiful and loving spouse. 2.2 darling children. Nice car. Nice house. Nice job. Nice boss. Just great.

However, now for the first time, we find life to be hard. Something has shattered our "heaven on earth." We wonder what we did to deserve this. We wonder why this is happening to us. We wonder why God is picking on us.

- We never asked those questions when life was great.
- We never asked, "What have I done to deserve this?" when sitting down to a sumptuous Thanksgiving dinner at Grandma's house.
- We never asked "What have I done to deserve this?" when voted most popular in school.

- We never asked "What have I done to deserve this?" when our complexion was clear while our friends' faces looked like a lunar surface.
- We never asked, "What have I done to deserve this?" when our spouse is loving and faithful and devoted.
- We never asked, "What have I done to deserve this?" when we were recruited for a new job and a great promotion, i.e. more money.

The "Why me?" and the "What did I do to make God angry?" and the "Who caused this?" questions were never asked then. But when trouble came they are the first questions on our mind. However, others of us have known considerable hardship.

- We were born with physical problems for which we had to learn to compensate.
- We are the children of divorced parents.
- We were abandoned by both parents at birth.
- We had to survive serious childhood diseases.
- We had to cope with tragedy in our family at a very young age.
- We had to survive rape and incest.
- We had to fight addictions that threatened to destroy us.
- We had to struggle in school.
- We had to sit at home on prom night.
- We had to work our way through school.
- We had to cope with an unfaithful spouse.
- We had to climb out of the pit of bankruptcy.

    Life has not been easy.

For us, hardship and suffering are not new. We understand life is not fair, difficulties come to every life, the rain falls on the just and the unjust. God's blessings are freely bestowed regardless of merit. Suffering is equally experienced regardless of guilt.

Jesus knew that. He clearly told us there would be some bad times, times of being poor in spirit, times of mourning, times of meekness, times of hunger and thirst, times of testing and even times of persecution. He clearly told us to expect hard times. They are part and parcel of life. Rough times come to every life, sooner or later.

That may come as unwelcome news to those of us who have had pretty good lives so far. But it is not news to many others.

It is not news to most people in this world. They know life is not fair. They know hardship comes to all, eventually. They know suffering is real in this life. They know depression. They know hopelessness. They know longing. They know pain. And they know all of us will someday know suffering, no matter how charmed our path may have been thus far.

Jesus knew that. When he spoke to the multitude gathered on the hillside beside the Sea of Galilee near Capernaum, he knew there were people in that crowd who had experienced the hardships of life. He also knew there were the privileged ones who had so far escaped the harsh realities of life. But he knew all would sooner or later know life is hard.

Given the reality of hard times in this life, Jesus told us how we ought to act. We are to be "poor in spirit," we are to "mourn," we are to "hunger and thirst for righteousness," we are to be "merciful," we are to be "pure in heart," we are to be "peacemakers," and we are to "rejoice and be glad."

Why? Because these are the actions and attributes necessary to enjoy the kingdom of heaven. These are necessary for comfort. These are necessary to inherit the earth. These are necessary for filling. These are necessary for receiving mercy. These are necessary to see God. These are necessary to be called children of God. These are necessary to receive a great reward in heaven.

Please be aware these are the actions and attributes that should accompany the life of a follower of Jesus Christ. We do not manufacture these on our own. They are the result of living in a close relationship with Jesus. They are the gift of grace in our lives. We don't do these things to earn our way into heaven. We do these things because they are true to our nature, the nature of Jesus.

We even endure persecution for Jesus' sake. Why? Because when we receive Jesus we begin to take on his nature. And as we grow in the grace of Jesus, we become more and more like Him, until we grow into the full stature of Christ.

Does that mean the hardships are not hard? Not at all. Does that mean the pain does not hurt? Not at all. Does that mean the meekness is not humbling. Not at all. Does that mean the poverty of spirit is not hard to swallow. Not at all. Does that mean the persecution does not sting. Not at all.

A number of years ago Bob Dylan wrote a song in which he was watching the verbal persecution of a Christian man take place:

"Go ahead and talk about him because he makes you doubt,
Because he's denied himself things that you can't do without,
Because he can't be exploited by superstition anymore,
Because he can't be bribed or bought by things that you adore.
He's the property of Jesus, resent him to the bone.
You've got something better---you've got a heart of stone.
When the whip that's keeping you in line doesn't make him jump,
Say he's hard of hearing, say that he's a chump.
Say he's out of step with reality as you try to test his nerve.
Because he doesn't pay tribute to the sovereign that you serve.

He's the property of Jesus, resent him to the bone.
You've got something better---you've got a heart of stone."

We respond to the hardship and the persecution the way we do as Christians because "Greater is he that is in you than he that is in the world." We rejoice in persecution because of Jesus "who for the joy that was set before him, endured the cross, despising the shame." We hunger and thirst for righteousness because righteousness is the nature of our Savior. We make peace because we know the Prince of Peace.

That ought to be enough. We ought to rejoice in suffering simply because we know Jesus. We ought to be poor in spirit simply because we know Jesus. We ought to be meek simply because we know Jesus. We ought to be meek because of Him. We ought to be pure in heart because of Jesus. We ought to make peace because we know Him.

However, Jesus loved us too much to leave it at that. No, we endure persecution, we make peace, we strive for purity, we show mercy, we hunger and thirst for righteousness, we mourn, we are poor in spirit because: "Great is your reward in Heaven."

You see, Jesus taught the reality of heaven. Heaven is real. Jesus made it clear that heaven is the reward for those whose lives are characteristic of the life of Jesus.

"On the night before he was crucified, Jesus told his disciples, "Let not you heart be troubled. You believe in God, believe also in me. In my Father's house are many mansions (mansions-KJV, rooms-RSV, condos-RWL). If it were not so, I would have told you I am going to prepare a place of you. And if I go and prepare a place for you, I will come again to receive you unto myself, that where I am you may be also. And where I go you know, and the way you know."

It was Thomas who said, "Lord, we do not know where you are going, how can we know the way?"

Jesus said, "I am the way, the truth and the life. No one comes to the Father except through me (John 14:1-6)."

Yes, Jesus wanted us to know after this life, after the joys and the sorrows, after the hopes and disappointments, after the happy times and the sad times of this life, Heaven awaits those who through faith come to Jesus, "the way, the truth and the life." Heaven – a place of eternal, everlasting joy and blessing.

Just what, then, will heaven be like? Have you ever wondered about heaven?

Here are some kids' ideas about what heaven is like:
One eight-year-old named Eric said, "It is a place where there is a lot of money lying around. You could just pick it up, play with it, and buy things. I think I am going to buy a basketball and I am going to play basketball with my great-great-grandmother."

Scott said, "Heaven is up in the sky, and you could look down at circuses for free if you want to, except you have to ask God for permission first."

Tommy, age seven said, "I know what heaven is, but I don't want to go there. I want to go to North Carolina instead" *(The Shepherd's Voice, Dec 16, 1979. From Autoillustrator.).*

What will heaven be like? Listen to the these words from the Book of Revelation (chapters 21 &22):

"And I heard a loud voice from the throne saying, 'Now the dwelling of God is with men, and he will live with them. They will be his people, and God himself will be with them and be their God. He will wipe every tear from their eyes. There will be no more death or mourning or crying or pain. For the old order of things has passed away.'" "Then the angel showed me the river of the water of life, as clear as crystal, flowing from the throne of God and of the Lamb. . .On each side of the river stood the tree of life. . .No longer will there be any curse. The throne of God and of the Lamb will be in the city, and his servants will serve him. They will see his face, and his name will be on their foreheads"

That is the greatest attempt in all of literature to capture the beauty, majesty and joy of heaven, an attempt to describe the indescribable. However, words cannot describe what God has prepared for his children. The Apostle Paul said it this way: "No eye has seen, no ear has heard, no mind has conceived what God has prepared for those who love him...(I Cor. 2:9).

While our temporal minds and temporal languages cannot conceive of or begin to describe heaven, we are assured of its reality and its absolute joy. It is a place where that which is lost is restored. It is a place where the sadness of this life is replaced with gladness. It is a place where rewards are distributed and great work is done. It is a place without the need for a sea, the earth's septic system. There is no pollution in heaven. It is a world without a sun. The Lamb of God provides all the light needed there. It is a world without suffering or pain. It is a world where we will live forever if we have been followers of The Way.

Describe it? I can't. But I know I will see my son again in heaven. I will wrap my arms around him and kiss him on the cheek. I will see my Daddy again in heaven. He won't be sick anymore. He will be like the Daddy I knew as a boy, only better. I will see my Mama and Papa Lathem and my Grandmother and Granddaddy Youngblood in heaven. And the list could go on and on.

One of the greatest thrills will be to see the people I got to lead to Jesus. And I am looking forward to meeting people I do not even know who were won to Christ through the ministries of the Seminario Wesleyano de Venezuela.

But most of all, I long to see Jesus. I want to fall on my face before Him and thank him for saving my soul. I want to sing praises to the Lamb. I want to worship with the great multitude, the Apostles, the Elders of the Twelve Tribes of Israel, the legions upon legions of Angels and join the mighty chorus, "Holy, Holy, Holy!"

What will it be like? I'm not sure. But I long for the day. Like a baby waiting to be born, snuggled safe in her mother's womb, life here on earth is a wonderful experience. But much more than we have ever dreamed or imagined waits on the other side. Like that unborn child, we can't even imagine its splendor. But far more awaits us on the other side than we have yet known or experienced.

What will Heaven be? I want to know, don't you?

Jesus is the Way.

I will follow Him. Come with me.

Chapter 6

Jesus Forgave the Adulterer
John 8:3-11

John 8:3 The teachers of the law and the Pharisees brought in a woman caught in adultery. They made her stand before the group 4 and said to Jesus, "Teacher, this woman was caught in the act of adultery. 5 In the Law Moses commanded us to stone such women. Now what do you say?" 6 They were using this question as a trap, in order to have a basis for accusing him. But Jesus bent down and started to write on the ground with his finger. 7 When they kept on questioning him, he straightened up and said to them, "If any one of you is without sin, let him be the first to throw a stone at her." 8 Again he stooped down and wrote on the ground. 9 At this, those who heard began to go away one at a time, the older ones first, until only Jesus was left, with the woman still standing there. 10 Jesus straightened up and asked her, "Woman, where are they? Has no one condemned you?" 11 "No one, sir," she said. "Then neither do I condemn you," Jesus declared. "Go now and leave your life of sin."

*****

Preachers have often been condemned for talking about sin all the time. We are called "Fire and Brimstone Preachers," narrow, closed minded, condemning and judgmental when we stoop to identify sin as sin. When we dare call sin what it is, we are condemned by this permissive society.

Well, today, that is just what many may do with this sermon. Every one of us has known someone whose life has been devastated because of adultery. However, as a pastor with 40 years' experience, I have seen more than any one person should have to see in a lifetime. Husbands, wives, children, parents, grandparents, grandchildren, aunts and uncles, friends, churches, businesses and communities torn apart because of adultery.

It is a horrible sin in its temporal consequences. The lasting devastation of adultery is hard to fathom. But it is certainly almost impossible to imagine when caught up in the lust of the moment.

No matter how we may want to minimize, rationalize or legitimize adultery, it is always wrong and it always has damaging consequences to a lot of people, especially the people closest to us. Betrayal, remorse, guilt, bitterness, self-loathing, misplaced priorities, and broken-ness always result from the selfish act of adultery. It is a devastating sin regardless of which side of the offense you are on. On one side is unending regret, the other is the sense of utter betrayal.

Charles Swindoll says it well: "According to the Old Testament law adultery required punishment by death, (Lev. 20:10). According to the teachings of Christ in the New Testament, it was legitimate grounds for divorce (Matthew 5:32). Can any sin be as painful, as far-reaching in its consequences, as difficult to forgive?"

Of the clandestine thrill of adultery, Solomon poetically writes: "Stolen water is sweet; and bread eaten in secret is pleasant" (Proverbs 9:17).

But in the very next verse, Solomon focuses on the tragic consequences of entering into such a relationship: "But he does not know that the dead are there, that her guests are in the depths of Sheol."

To recognize the devastating implications of adultery is one thing. Then to condemn the person guilty of such sin is something else altogether. For the woman in John 8, caught in the very act of adultery, her life, too, would never be the same again. Not because of the stones of judgment ready to be cast at her by the self-righteous crowd of Pharisees, but because of the soft words of forgiveness spoken to her by Jesus.

The story of the woman caught in adultery is intriguing. We are fascinated by the way Jesus handled this situation and fascinated by what we can learn.

This passage reveals the true heart of judgmental people. The Pharisees and Scribes present themselves as those supremely concerned for God's law. But our passage shows this was not the case. If they had really been concerned for the law they would have brought both parties who were "caught" as the law commanded. Isn't it interesting how these self-righteous men chose only to condemn the woman, while ignoring the actions of her partner? I guess the old adage, "Boys will be boys," was known in Jesus' day as well.

However, isn't this indicative of how we condemn the sins of others and excuse our own? Isn't this how we judge others and excuse folks who act like us? Isn't this indicative of how society has treated women and excused the actions of men?

This is true of those today who wag their bony fingers in our faces. They swell up as if they were defending God's honor but this is deceptive. If they were truly concerned about God's law they would be concerned about the command to "Judge Not! (Matt. 7:1)."

The real concern of those religious leaders was to trap Jesus. They wanted to put him on the "horns of a dilemma." If he says, "stone her" then he has trouble with the Roman Government for commanding an illegal killing. He also puts his own integrity in jeopardy. After all, Jesus spent time with tax-collectors and sinners. And if he says "Don't stone her" he appears to disregard the law of God.

The real concern of those who are judgmental is not to help us find grace . . . it is to increase our misery. We must never become soft on sin. We must be clear that certain things are wrong but…our focus is to be redemptive…not punitive. The judgmental seek to be judgmental, not helpful.

Not only were these men looking for a way to trap Jesus, they were looking for a way to exalt themselves. You see, Jesus was a threat to their territory. He was causing people to ask embarrassing questions, to leave the "fold." They could not allow this to continue or they might never recover. By tearing down Jesus they hoped to elevate themselves.

This is true of the judgmental of today. For some reason there is a perverted sense that by tearing down another we are exalting ourselves. Maybe it is because when others are in the spotlight we are not.

The pretense is a person is doing something spiritual. However, in reality when we are judging others we are engaging in the most worldly of pursuits. We are playing God.

So, how do we combat this tendency? What is the antidote to a judgmental attitude? It's really quite simple: Look at yourself in the mirror. We must realize that the person who has fallen is different from us only in the fact that they have fallen and we haven't …yet!

About 30 years ago I was leading the singing at Pinelog
Campmeeting. Bevel Jones was the preacher. This was long
before he became a Bishop. News reached us of a preacher's
disgrace in an illicit affair. After discussing the tragedy, Bevel
said, "There but for the grace of God go I - yet!

I was stunned. Bevel's reputation was beyond reproach. He went
on to be elected bishop. He was an old man – at least over 50.
How could he think he could do something like that? Well I am
older and I have learned that any one of us is capable of anything
at any time.

We are no better than anyone else. Our sin may not be as obvious
as theirs may or as socially reprehensible, but we are still sinners.

Often I will hear someone say, "I like you as a preacher but I have
problems with some of the members of your congregation…you
see, I know them. They aren't very holy out in the real world."

That's like saying, "I like the hospital but it always seems to have
sick people in it!" Let me ask, "Where are sinful people supposed
to go?" This attitude of being better than each other is un-
Christian and very unbecoming.

What is the best way to stimulate holy living? Surprisingly, Jesus
does not condemn this woman. He tells her that He does not
condemn her.

We are tempted to say, "Jesus let her off…that will just encourage
her to sin more." But if so, we miss the point. Jesus does not
minimize her sin, not at all. And neither should we.

- Adultery, regardless of circumstances, is wrong.
- Perverted lifestyles are an abomination to the Lord.
- Gossip offends God's holiness.

- Theft builds a wall of separation between us and God.
- Prejudice is reprehensible to the Father.
- Superficial religion disgusts God.

The list could go on. We must be Biblical about the sinfulness of sin. But, at the same time we must realize that while sin is horrible, the sinner is invited to come for forgiveness. We are not the judge, God is the judge. We do not have all the facts ... God does. We cannot judge impartially...God can ...and does.

We also need to realize adultery is not the unpardonable sin. Jesus makes that most clear in this passage, "Neither do I condemn you, go and sin no more." We have often branded the adulterer with the Scarlet Letter, as if there could be no forgiveness, no restoration, no salvation. How totally unfair and anti-scriptural! Jesus offers forgiveness and restoration to the adulterer.

Now there are times when people do not see the sin in their lives. Those people must be shown their sin before they can be introduced to mercy. However, most of the time sinful people are well aware of our sinfulness. We don't need someone to jump on our body once we have been mugged by sin . . . we need someone to lend us a hand so we can get up!

Some might also argue that Jesus' response to this woman will encourage her to take lightly the pursuit of holiness. I disagree.

There is nothing like getting a taste of the freedom that comes from mercy. One taste of that freedom and we don't want to go back.

This woman didn't leave Jesus feeling she "got away with something." She left feeling blessed beyond words.

I love the words of Ken Gire in his book INTIMATE MOMENTS: "There are no tears as she leaves. Years later there will be. At odd moments during the day: when she looks at her children asleep in their beds; when she waves good-bye to her husband as he walks to work in the morning; when she kneads bread in the solitude of her kitchen," then she will cry, cry tears of thanksgiving and gratitude for what mercy has brought about.

A marriage she never would have had...a family she never would have had...a life she never would have had - were it not for such a wonderful Savior, a Savior who stood up for her when others wanted to stone her. A Savior who stooped to pick her up and send her on her way, forgiven.

No, this woman did not take the gift for granted. This love motivated her just like it motivates everyone who has tasted such limitless forgiveness and grace.

The question I pose is this: With whom in this story do you most identify?

Are you going through life with clenched fists: one clenching an accusing point and the other a rock? It may not be a literal stone but it may be a rock of slander, a rock of innuendo, a rock of disapproval. Are you trying to "grow" spiritually by tearing others down? If so, it is time to repent of your foolishness. Stop looking at others and look in the mirror. It's time for you to deal with YOUR sin, my friend.

Or perhaps you feel like the woman...everywhere you go you feel the stares. You sense everyone whispering about you. You know you have fallen... you know you have made mistakes. You wish you could go back and make some decisions differently.

If this is you, I remind you that there is one who is more concerned about restoring your life than taking it. There is one more concerned about healing than increasing your pain. His name is Jesus. Turn to Him . . . He knows what you have done and He will forgive you and set you free if you will turn to Him.

Or perhaps you identify most closely with the missing person in this scripture text: the adulterous man who seems to have gotten away with it. There are many of you n the church. I know because I know the people of the church. You were the undiscovered party in an adulterous relationship. It has not been revealed. You have escaped everything except the guilt and shame and the knowledge of God.

Unlike the adulterous woman who was exposed, your sin is hidden, except from you and God. You know and God knows. But because it is hidden, there can be no redemption, no experience of grace and mercy. Until you own it before God, you will live with the horrible guilt and shame.

Someone will ask, "Then should I tell my spouse?" If he or she doesn't know about it and if it will injure him or her, do not tell. However, tell Jesus and go to a counselor or a pastor to get help with understanding what caused such damaging behavior and how you can insure it won't happen again.

And there are some today who are currently engaged in an adulterous relationship. Get out of it! Now! Don't wait for even more harm to come.

Free yourself from the grip of sin.

Jesus will help you.

Chapter 7

Jesus Forgave the Persecutor
Luke 23:26-34a

26 As they led him away, they seized Simon from Cyrene, who was on his way in from the country, and put the cross on him and made him carry it behind Jesus. 27 A large number of people followed him, including women who mourned and wailed for him. 28 Jesus turned and said to them, "Daughters of Jerusalem, do not weep for me; weep for yourselves and for your children. 29 For the time will come when you will say, `Blessed are the barren women, the wombs that never bore and the breasts that never nursed!'  30  Then  "`they will say to the mountains, "Fall on us!" and to the hills, "Cover us!" ' 31 For if men do these things when the tree is green, what will happen when it is dry?" 32 Two other men, both criminals, were also led out with him to be executed. 33 When they came to the place called the Skull, there they crucified him, along with the criminals--one on his right, the other on his left. 34 Jesus said, "Father, forgive them, for they do not know what they are doing."

*****

Jesus forgave the persecutor. Listen to his words on the cross of Calvary: "Father, forgive them, for they do not know what they are doing."

Jesus was familiar with persecution. From the very beginning of his ministry, the political, economic and religious leaders were after him. They saw him as a threat to their position and their status. While a significant part of the threat was religious, the greatest threat was economic. Privilege and power always have economic implications.

When Jesus invested himself with the poor and marginalized of his society, he created a threat to the economic stability of the power structure of Palestine. Therefore, from the beginning, they were out to get him.

And they got him. Or so it seemed to them. They finally got him accused of a crime, tried, convicted and executed. But just before he died he took the power of their hate and persecution away from them when he prayed, "Father, forgive them, for they do not know what they are doing."

Jesus was aware that both he and his followers would experience persecution. What did he have to say about it?

First of all, he said to expect it. Remember how he said, "In this world you will have persecution?" That is pretty clear. There are forces opposed to the work and will of God in providing redemption and liberation for his people.

There are enemies to the work of God in the world. There is no question of that. If you are not personally aware of the work of evil, then you have not entered into the work of redemption God is doing in the world. Take up the cross and you will experience persecution, opposition, abuse, ridicule, and shame. That is simply the result of living a Christian life in a pagan culture.

However, there is a greater power at work against the work of the kingdom than just the mores of the culture. It is embodied in Satan himself. Lucifer. The Devil. Old Slewfoot. There is one who is the Prince of Darkness. He rules the forces of evil and he brings his minions to the task of thwarting the purposes of God.

Years ago I learned to warn my staff and lay leaders to get ready for the opposition of Satan. I discovered anytime we made a major move which would result in people coming to Christ, opposition would come, demonic opposition, and usually from the place or persons we least expected. So I would warn my lay leaders and staff to get ready. What did I warn them to get ready for? The attack of Satan. I knew that if we were serious about reaching others with the Gospel of Jesus Christ, Satan would come after us. I did not know how or when or where. I just knew it would happen.

Since then several things have occurred that have caused others to proclaim that my words were in fact prophetic. Opposition, diabolical transactions, evil forces have struck again and again. Why? Because there is an Evil One who is determined to undermine and destroy the work of redemption in the world.

We have seen this played out in very tangible ways over and over in Venezuela. In fact, on our most recent trip we experienced such a violent attack that except for the grace of God it could have ended our work in Venezuela. It was inexplicable, unless one realized the potent opposition present to thwart the work of redemption. However, we are thankful to say, "The Battle Belongs to the Lord!"

Martin Luther wrote:
> *And though this world, with devils filled, should threaten to undo us,*
> *We will not fear, for God hath willed His truth to triumph through us:*
> *The Prince of Darkness grim, we tremble not for him;*
> *His rage we can endure, for lo, his doom is sure,*
> *One little word shall fell him.*

There is a spiritual battle going on in this world. The Evil one seeks to destroy the redemptive work of God.

Observation: the reason most Christians in most churches in the US do not experience, much less even believe in, spiritual warfare is they are not engaged in the battle. If one is reaching no one for Christ, then one will not experience the attack of Satan. Spiritual warfare is real only to those engaged in the battle. The battle is for the eternal redemption of the lost. Most Christians and churches in the US reach almost no one with the saving and transforming gospel of Jesus Christ. Just look at the statistics - especially among my fellow UM's. In Venezuela, the battle is real, because real people are being redeemed by the blood of Jesus.

This Evil One thought he had won when they nailed Jesus to the cross. But before Jesus would die, there was the sign of the triumph of the Gospel over the forces of evil, when he said, "Father, forgive them, for they do not know what they are doing."

Don't you hate it when you are mean and rotten and cruel to someone and all they do is forgive you! They won't fight. They won't strike back. They won't retaliate. Oh! How much we would rather fight to the finish. No holds barred. Tooth and nail thrown into the fray. But they don't fight back. They just forgive you. It takes all the power out of your evil action and your evil intent, doesn't it?

Those words of forgiveness spoken by Jesus on the cross were just the precursor to the resurrection. Evil would not win. The persecutor would not triumph. Injustice would not reign supreme. Jesus rose from the dead! And his resurrection is God's word of redemption, hope, triumph and power over the forces of persecution and evil.

Jesus told us to expect persecution. But he went further. He told us to rejoice in it.

Listen to his words in Matthew 5:11-12; "Blessed are you when people insult you, persecute you and falsely say all kinds of evil against you because of me. Rejoice and be glad, because great is your reward in heaven, for in the same way they persecuted the prophets who were before you."

"Rejoice!" "Rejoice!" What in the world is Jesus talking about? Listen to him carefully: *"...against you because of me."* There is no higher privilege for the Christian than to be numbered with Jesus, to be associated with Jesus, than to be identified with Jesus.

He was the "man of sorrows and acquainted with grief." Can his followers expect the world to treat them any differently than it treated him? Can the disciple of Jesus expect Satan to deal with him or her any differently than he dealt with Jesus?

No! If you take seriously the call of Jesus Christ upon your life and attempt to live in radical obedience to him, you will experience opposition and persecution. Rejoice! Rejoice! You are identified with Jesus!

You see, Jesus said persecution is a source of blessing. Listen to him in Matthew 5:10; "Blessed are those who are persecuted because of righteousness, for theirs is the kingdom of heaven."

Jesus said expect persecution, rejoice in persecution because it is a source of blessing. What did Jesus do about persecution?

First of all, he was not surprised by it. Isn't it amazing how surprising it is to us when persecution comes our way? We aren't expecting it. Why? Usually we are not living in such radical obedience to the Father's will as to make ourselves the objects of persecution. We are working so hard to fit in, to just be one of the men and women in the neighborhood that we are indistinguishable from the world. Then persecution comes and we cry out, "What did I do to deserve this?"

The truth is, often we have done nothing, except align ourselves with the cause of Christ. Far too often it is not because of our sacrificial service, our self-denying giving, our passion for the lost and the lonely. We know those things result in persecution. That's why we shy away from them!

If we are following Jesus with integrity, we should not be surprised by persecution. We also should not let it make us bitter.

You see, in spite of being persecuted, Jesus did not let it make him a bitter person. Hear him again, "Father forgive them, for they do not know what they are doing." No bile. No bitterness. No need to retaliate.

If Jesus did not get bitter because of persecution, if he did not drown in the bile of persecution, if he did not retaliate against those who opposed and persecuted him, what did he do?

Jesus prayed for the persecutor. Listen to his words: "Father, forgive them, for they do not know what they are doing." That is a prayer. He is praying for those specific persons who were responsible for his suffering.

It is absolutely amazing how powerful prayer can be. It can transform the one who is prayed for, but it can also transform the one who does the praying. I have experienced the power of praying for my enemies. It is one of the most liberating things have ever experienced. It takes all the power out of their harmful, hateful, evil actions. Prayer simply takes away the sting.

But Jesus did more than pray. He forgave them. His words on the cross are words of forgiveness.

Now, that is tough. But Jesus did it. And the Bible reminds us that we can do it too: "But I tell you, love your enemies and pray for those who persecute you," (Matthew 5:44). If Jesus forgave the persecutor, so can we, those of us who name the name of Jesus.

So far this sermon has been all about when we are persecuted. But now let's turn the tables a little bit and talk about when we are the persecutor. That's right, I said when we are the persecutor.

Do you ever find yourself in that role, the role of the persecutor? Before you say, "No," let's look a little closer.

For what have you ever persecuted another? Their faith? No? Ever made fun of Pentecostal Christians calling them, "Holy Rollers?" Ever ridiculed Jews by referencing a stereotype? Ever disparaged Catholics calling them, "Mackerel Snappers." Ever laughed at the cold formalism of Episcopalians? Ever spoken of "Rag Heads" when referring to Moslems?

Have you ever persecuted another because of their values? Maybe their sexual orientation is not acceptable to you or God, but you went beyond that acknowledgment to committing acts of violence or discrimination or hate against them. Perhaps you think violence against a gynecologist who will perform an abortion is justifiable. Perhaps you have turned your head when you have seen another ridiculed and persecuted because their values did not mesh with those of you and others around you.

What about race? I was having lunch with a fellow UMC pastor. He told me about a restaurant in Alpharetta where he can hardly get service. He said the staff will just ignore his presence. I was surprised. I have eaten in that restaurant several times. I've always received excellent service. I couldn't imagine my fellow pastor not getting the same service. Except for the fact that he is black and I am white, what difference could there be?

Now, I know that we are too enlightened to make disparaging remarks and treat with disdain and persecution someone of African-American descent. After all, we are Christians.

Recently, the Bishop told me about a church in southwest Atlanta. The community is almost completely black. The Methodist church is completely white. They drive in from other communities to go to church there. The Bishop wanted to appoint a black pastor there to help the church reach out to its community. One of the long time members, a former lay leader, was indignant and said, "We've already given our hospital, our schools and our campground to the _____ (N word). I'll be damned if we're going to give 'em our church, too!"

Oh, I know we would never say anything like that, would we? But let me tell you, the next person I hear say anything of a disparaging nature about Mexicans or Hispanics, I'm going to back-hand them across the mouth. Jesus forgave the persecutor. In case you hadn't noticed, I'm not Jesus! Just kidding. I won't back-hand anyone. I will just want too.

What about persecution because of status or class? None of us is guilty of that, are we? This persecution, this prejudice, for prejudice is persecution, can be toward those who are above us or those we perceive to be below us.

How many times have I heard people talk about those people who are so uppity they live behind guarded gates? And how often I have heard those of us who live in this community speak despairingly of the poor and the uneducated.

You say, "Not me!" Are you sure? Where do you bury your garbage? In your own back yard? Or do you have it hauled off to be buried in someone else's back yard? Do you ever buy imported goods from Mexico? Why? They are cheaper. Why are they cheaper? Because Mexican workers will work to make stuff for you and me, and they will work for far less than we will work for. Also, there are almost no governmental controls on pollution in Mexico. So their factories are spewing our pollutants at such a rate that Mexico City has become one of the most polluted cities in the world – just to make stuff to sell to you and me. We don't breathe the air of Mexico, so why should we care?

When we disparage those who serve us, we are guilty of persecution. I am aware that is a hard word and an unpopular concept in these economic and political times, but it is still true.

But there is good news. Jesus forgives the persecutor. However, the experience of forgiveness requires acknowledgment of sin and repentance from sin, a turning from sin.

What is it that the Holy Spirit is calling to your attention today for which you need to repent? Do you need to forgive the persecutor? Do you need to be forgiven of your own persecution of others because of your prejudice or gossip or hatred?

Jesus forgave the persecutor. He will forgive you.

Can you receive that forgiveness? Can you forgive?

Chapter 8

Jesus Forgave the Thief
Luke 23:39-43

Luke 23:39 One of the criminals who hung there hurled insults at him: "Aren't you the Christ? Save yourself and us!" 40 But the other criminal rebuked him. "Don't you fear God," he said, "since you are under the same sentence? 41 We are punished justly, for we are getting what our deeds deserve. But this man has done nothing wrong." 42 Then he said, "Jesus, remember me when you come into your kingdom." 43 Jesus answered him, "I tell you the truth, today you will be with me in paradise."

******

The moment of approaching death - sometimes it comes quickly, totally unexpected. But sometimes we see it coming, standing at the bedside of a loved one who has grown feeble with age, or whose body has been ravaged by disease. The end of earthly life is certain. We can sense it. The body grows weaker; pulse flutters; breathing intermittent. We prepare for that inevitable moment of having to let go. We don't want to. We hang on while we can. But then we realize there is no choice.

They will leave. Leave to where? Where do we go when we die? When do we go there? Who goes where?

These are some of the great questions of life. We ignore these questions until those power-filled moments, when they come roaring out of the back room where we have stuffed them. They come roaring out and by-passing all the other stuff of mortgage payments, football games, vacation planning and career advancement. All those other things that seemed so incredibly important quickly fade into something next to irrelevance.

These are the questions you assume can wait until you're 80-something. They can wait until - until that phone call comes just after midnight, or the doctor asks us to get our family together so she can talk to us, or the police and the social worker show up at our door.

Some of you know what I'm talking about. You've been there. You've buried your school classmates before they had a chance to graduate. Some of you have buried children that you expected would bury you. Some have had a colleague at work who had such a promising career ahead. Some of you have stood at the graveside of the one you thought would be there for life. Only her life ended way too soon.

You know that questions about death and what lies beyond death cannot be stuffed into "the back 40 acres" to wait for whenever. You know questions of life and death and salvation and eternity demand an answer.

Today we are transported by the Bible to the scene of 3 persons preparing to leave the experience of life as we know it here on earth. Their bodies will expire and their souls will move on.
- to what?
- where?
- who?
- and when?

It is a place of execution. There is Jesus. And there are two others - criminals, they are called. We're not told what the crime was. We have traditionally called them thieves. It doesn't matter. Criminals. That's all. Guilty. Period. The punishment for their crime would have to be exacted. Justice demanded it be so. Payment for the wrong committed.

Three men, gasping, groaning, in pain, life dripping out onto the ground. Torture. Public humiliation. Somehow, through all that, with the clock running down.... somehow there is time for an exchange between them. Even while the horizon becomes less focused, and the pain overwhelms the three engage in conversation. We are quiet witnesses of this sacred moment.

One criminal is defiant! To the end he'll be strong. He won't give in to the humiliating taunts thrown his way. He won't surrender to the embarrassment of being hung out to die stark naked in front of a crowd. He'll keep the tough guy image. The shell won't crack. So while he still can, he turns his barbs onto his fellow sufferer, the one in the middle.

Maybe we admire that -- at least for the moment. We live in a country that's been built on the tough, resourceful, independent pioneer & immigrant spirit. We admire that kind of guy. He would have made Clint Eastwood proud. He would have knocked Sylvester Stallone down a peg or two. He would have made "tough-guy" Bruce Willis stand and salute.

But, as plain as day, we can see there's something beyond the moment. He'll gasp his last breath. And then what? Toss his body in a pauper's grave. That we know. But what of his soul -- that eternal part of him which no one on earth can kill? We begin to think about that and we start to feel restless.

So we turn to the other side. Another criminal. But this one's not so loud, so brash. He's quiet. He, too, is focused on the one in the middle. He's not so cocky, so angry, so bitter. He's watching. And only then, after some time, does he speak. First to the guy on the far end, trying desperately to knock some sense into him, to get him to drop his Rambo image and face the inevitable. Tragically, it doesn't work.

Then he turns his attention to the one in the middle. He's been watching him; watching Jesus. He saw how he was different. Innocent. That was obvious from the word "go." But there's much more. How much of that "much more" this criminal saw we don't know. The Bible doesn't really say. We're left to speculate. But we do see, through the lens of scripture, what he sees. We hear what he hears.

He sees a man without violence praying, "Father, forgive them, for they do not know what they are doing." And somehow something clicks. It comes together. God, as father. Forgiveness. Everyone's heard the claims of this man -- to be Messiah, to be God's son. Could it be?

And those words, "forgive them for they do not know what they are doing." He understands. But are they for him?

It's a desperate moment. This man's a criminal. He knows it. His time is limited. Just a few hours. He's approaching the edge and will soon tumble over. God and judgment await. He knows that, too.

Desperate moments call for desperate actions. So this desperate man, convicted criminal, finds the words - "Jesus, remember me when you come into your kingdom."

Remember me when you come into your kingdom.
There's a huge confession there -- that Jesus would be living beyond this cross. The confession was that the cross for Jesus was the entrance to power in a kingdom beyond the bricks and mortar of this world.

Jesus - when you come there, could there be, maybe a little corner for me? Jesus - when you come there, please don't abandon me to eternal darkness, to being a wandering soul with no place to go, or a soul in eternal torment. Jesus - mercy!

"Today you will be with me in Paradise," Jesus said.

> No "maybe, we'll see."
> No "someday."
> No "why should I?"
> And definitely no "absolutely not!"

Instead – "Today you will be with me in Paradise." It was an absolute guarantee served up in a moment.

The convict relaxes. No more is said. No more needs to be said. It's okay. Eternally okay.

Can you see that scene as it plays itself out? Burn it into your memory. It is one of crucial importance to your future. There's an enormous message for each one of us here this morning.

For, you see, we're really not a lot different than that convicted con. You know the biggest difference? He got caught. His crime is not identified. He wears a generic label: "criminal." It is a label that could have your name or mine written on it.

Convicted -- and condemned. We have committed an offense which justice demands be punished. Isn't that you and me, from God's point of view?

Is there any one of us here who can say with a straight face that we've lived a perfect life and always done what God required? Everyday? Can we say we have avoided what He wants us to avoid? Have we thought, spoke and done what He desired? Did we keep Him at that central place in life where He belongs?

In God's eyes we are exactly the same as the criminal on the cross: GUILTY, CONVICTED, CONDEMNED, the execution is being carried out – DEATH. Eternal justice screams that we must be condemned to eternal death.

Three men died on a cross that day. Which one are you?

Look at the first man. He died in his sin (Luke 23:39).

Even though he was confronted with his own helplessness, his own mortality, his own eternal destiny, he maintained his self-absorption until the very end. He was a sinner and he would die a sinner. No cry for mercy. No need for grace. No humility. No faith. No hope. No help.

Folks, I have seen so many people die just like this man. So many who had been in the presence of Jesus, but who refused to admit any need, refused to call upon him, refused to come to the end of themselves. And they died in their sin.

Their way of life is described by Paul in Ephesians 2:1-2 "And you were dead in your trespasses and sins, in which you formerly walked according to the course of this world, according to the prince of the power of the air, of the spirit that is now working in the sons of disobedience."

To all of us like this man Jesus says, "I said therefore to you, that you shall die in your sins; for unless you believe that I am He, you shall die in your sins (John 8:24)." He says further, "I tell you, no, but unless you repent, you will all likewise perish (Luke 13:3)."

The writer of the New Testament book of Hebrews said, "It is appointed unto all once to die and then comes judgment (9:27)."

To die in sin is to face sure condemnation and eternal separation from God. To die in one's sins is to be eternally lost. To die in one's sins is to reject the Sweet Savior's offer of forgiveness and salvation.

A second man died on the cross that day. He died to sin (Luke 23; 40-42).

Not long before, this man, too, had hurled verbal venom at Jesus. But eternity dawned on him. Death's cold hand touched him. Judgment came to mind. And he repented. He died to sin.

Paul reminds all who have believed in Christ, "Therefore consider the members of your earthly body as dead to immorality, impurity, passion, evil desire, and greed, which amounts to idolatry. For it is on account of these things that the wrath of God will come, and in them you also once walked, when you were living in them. But now you also, put them all aside: anger, wrath, malice, slander, and abusive speech from your mouth. Do not lie to one another, since you laid aside the old self with its evil practices," Colossians 3:5-9.

It means that we loathe sin instead of loving it.
It means that we exterminate sin instead of excusing it.
It means that we deplore sin instead of defending it.
It means that we reject sin instead of rationalizing it.
It means that we incapacitate sin instead of indulging it.
It means that we crucify sin instead of coddling it.

Our attitude ought to be that expressed by the psalmist, "The sacrifices of God are a broken spirit; A broken and a contrite heart, O God, Thou wilt not despise (Psalm 51:17)."

If you've died to sin, you won't be living in it anymore; it won't rule you and you will have a broken and contrite heart. Your life will have changed.

One man's life was changed on the cross that day. It was the man who died to sin. And his eternal destiny was irrevocably changed.

A third man died on a cross that day. He died for sin (Luke 23:34, 46).

Jesus was not the victim of circumstances, a helpless martyr caught up in a plan gone awry! He was a willing participant and willingly clutched his own destiny!

Listen to His words:
"For this reason the Father loves me, because I lay down my life that I may take it again. No one has taken it away from me, but I lay it down on my own initiative. I have authority to lay it down, and I have authority to take it up again. This commandment I received from my Father (John. 10:17-18)."

Hear this:

Isaiah (53:6) said, "All of us like sheep have gone astray, Each of us has turned to his own way; But the Lord has caused the iniquity of us all to fall on Him."

Paul said, (2 Corinthians 5:21) "He made Him who knew no sin to be sin on our behalf, that we might become the righteousness of God in Him."

Again he said, (2 Corinthians 8:9) "For you know the grace of our Lord Jesus Christ, that though He was rich, yet for your sake He became poor, that you through His poverty might become rich."

And the Apostle Peter wrote: (1 Peter 2:24) "and He Himself bore our sins in His body on the cross, that we might die to sin and live to righteousness; for by His wounds you were healed."

God allowed Jesus to go to the Cross on our behalf, in our stead, "for the demonstration, I say, of His righteousness at the present time, that He might be just and the justifier of the one who has faith in Jesus," according to Paul (Romans 3:26).

So, Jesus died for sin and gave us a choice. The choice is limited to this: will you die in sin, or will you die to sin? Only you can decide that and your decision determines your destiny!

But carefully hear Jesus again on this matter: "I said therefore to you, that you shall die in your sins; for unless you believe that I am He, you shall die in your sins (John 8:24)."

But I do not want you to miss the Good News. Paul said it this way: "But God, being rich in mercy, because of His great love with which He loved us, even when we were dead in our transgressions, made us alive together with Christ (by grace you have been saved), and raised us up with Him, and seated us with Him in the heavenly places, in Christ Jesus, in order that in the ages to come He might show the surpassing riches of His grace in kindness toward us in Christ Jesus (Ephesians 2:4-7)."

Today may be your "wake-up call" to grace. After all, "Amazing love, how can it be, that Thou my God shouldst die for me?" (Charles Wesley).

Which one are you? The one destined to die in your sins?

Or are you the one who will die to sin?

The One who died for sin gives you the choice.

Chapter 9

Jesus Died To Self
Philippians 2:1-8

Philippians 2:1 If you have any encouragement from being united
with Christ, if any comfort from his love, if any fellowship with
the Spirit, if any tenderness and compassion, 2 then make my joy
complete by being like-minded, having the same love, being one in
spirit and purpose. 3 Do nothing out of selfish ambition or vain
conceit, but in humility consider others better than yourselves. 4
Each of you should look not only to your own interests, but also to
the interests of others. 5 Your attitude should be the same as that
of Christ Jesus: 6 Who, being in very nature God, did not
consider equality with God something to be grasped, 7 but made
himself nothing, taking the very nature of a servant, being made
in human likeness. 8 And being found in appearance as a man, he
humbled himself and became obedient to death-- even death on a
cross!

*****

In these poetic lines we discover three things about Christ: who he
is, what he has done in our behalf, what our attitude toward him
ought to be.

LET'S UNDERSTAND, FIRST OF ALL, WHO HE IS.

Many of us would like to straddle the fence at this point.
Intellectually, we count ourselves among the Trinitarians. We
gladly embrace the language--Father, Son and Holy Ghost--but
deep in our hearts we are reluctant to make an all-out commitment
to the divinity of Jesus. We consider the moral superiority of his

teachings beyond question. The picture he gives us of God is one we would like the whole world to embrace. The love which he taught and personified we understand surpasses any other love we have ever known.

Still, we want to lump him with other religious leaders like Confucius, Mohammed, and Moses. We cannot allow ourselves to acknowledge him as Lord. That is too much to ask of us intellectually. That a baby born to a Jewish peasant girl in a stable in the tiny town of Bethlehem could in fact be God is beyond our intellectual comprehension. That Jesus was in fact the eternal, pre-existent, all powerful God, Creator, Sustainer, Redeemer, when he was brutally nailed to a Roman cross is a concept most difficult to swallow. Are we to believe that the beaten, bruised body his friends removed from the cross and placed in a cold, dark tomb was in fact the earthly remains of God? That's quite an intellectual leap. That is a lot to ask, for us to believe that.

Even more important, it is too much to ask of us spiritually. If he truly is Lord, it would be impossible for us to keep him safely at arm's length. Acknowledging him as Lord will require too much from us--not only of our minds, but also our hearts. If Jesus is Lord of all, we can no longer ignore his claims on our lives. If Jesus is Lord, we can no longer live for ourselves. If Jesus is Lord, we can no longer ignore the pressing need of a world lost in spiritual darkness, dying to hear about the marvelous grace of Jesus.

If Jesus is Lord, then I am not. You are not. I am compelled, you are compelled, to bow before him in complete and absolute surrender to his Lordship in our lives. Yet this is the bold contention of our faith. Jesus is more than mere humanity. He is part of the Triune God. Jesus IS Lord!

Dorothy Sayers had one of the simplest and most helpful
explanations of the puzzling doctrine of the Trinity I have
discovered. She uses the example of a book. She notes that at first
the book is only an idea in its author's mind. Then it becomes a
book that you can hold and read and study. As you begin to grasp
and comprehend its ideas and to put its precepts into action,
however, it becomes something else. It takes on a kind of life of
its own in your mind. So, one work, but in three forms--idea,
book, and realization in the reader's mind.

Christians believe that God also manifests Himself in three forms--
God in His Divine essence, God in the historical person of Jesus,
and God, the Holy Spirit, who is the inward witness of Himself.
Therefore, we can see how Paul could describe Christ as "being in
the form of God..." and thinking "it not robbery to be equal with
God..." That is who he is. We need to focus on who Jesus is.

WE ALSO NEED TO UNDERSTAND WHAT HE HAS DONE
IN OUR BEHALF.

The Apostle Paul tells us he "took upon him the form of a servant,
and was made in the likeness of men: and being found in the
fashion of man he humbled himself and became obedient unto
death, even the death of the cross...."

In his immortal work, PARADISE LOST, Milton tells us about an
angel who sought to be equal with God. For this he was cast out of
heaven and now reigns in hell. These are the words Milton
attributed to Satan, "Better to reign in hell than to serve in heaven."
Note the difference between Satan and Christ. Paul describes
Christ as One who does not strive to be equal with God, but rather
humbles himself to the level of humanity, who becomes a servant,
and finally dies like a common thief.

Even more he humbled himself upon the cross. The beloved Christ was stripped of his dignity, forsaken by his friends, broken in body, if not in spirit. And he did it on our behalf.

In a Peanuts cartoon, Charlie Brown and Linus are standing next to each other, staring at a star-filled sky. "Would you like to see a falling star?" Charlie Brown asks Linus. "Sure..." Linus responds. "Then again, I don't know," he adds, after some thought. "I'd hate to have it fall just on my account."

In the book PARABLES OF PEANUTS, Robert Short uses this cartoon to make the point that a star did fall on our account. God came down to us as Jesus: like a lamb led to slaughter, He died on our account. What humility! What love! And, oh, what he accomplished there!

Back in 1927 a man named Asibi, a West African native, was stricken with the deadly disease, yellow fever. However, Asibi lived. Because his system had conquered the disease, Asibi's blood contained the antibodies from which to begin to develop a successful vaccine.

Today doctors and drug companies have developed an efficient vaccine against yellow fever, and their cure has saved the lives of untold numbers of people around the world. Each dose of vaccine, though, can be traced back to one original blood sample--that of Asibi. Literally, one man's blood saved the lives of millions of people.

In a mysterious way we cannot understand, that is exactly what the blood of Jesus Christ did for us. "By his stripes, we are been healed." We see who Christ is and what he has done in our behalf.

Paul tells us our response should look like this: "Your attitude should be the same as that of Christ Jesus." What does that mean?

1. Humility.

Humility is something we know very little about in this nation. A President can face the cameras, the eye of the nation, and tell us a bold-faced lie and not be humble enough to admit his wrong-doing even when the video records reveal the lies.

All of this would not be so upsetting if it were not reflective of a culture that has lost any sense of personal humility. We are a nation addicted to power, prestige, and position. We are a nation that has lost its will to humble itself before God. For this nation, God is a wonderful, warm and fuzzy idea, a cosmic stamp of approval for whatever we want to do in this life. This god we have created is a god who requires nothing, expects nothing, denies nothing and judges nothing.

If Jesus humbled himself, who are we to stand defiantly before the God of Salvation and deny him his rightful place in our lives – that of Lord and Master? There is no other appropriate response to the Lordship of Jesus Christ than that of the bended knee and the bowed heart. In genuine humility we must surrender to the Lordship of Jesus Christ.

Have you surrendered your life to Jesus? Have you claimed him as your Savior and Lord? There is no other appropriate response to him. Humility before Jesus. Humility and Servanthood.

2. Servanthood.

If Jesus is Lord and if we are to have the mind in us that was in Jesus, we will immediately become aware that we too, must become a servant. If the Lord of life became a servant to give us salvation, we must become his servant in a lost and dying world.

Dr. Eddie Fox is a good friend and President of the Institute of World Methodist Evangelism. Not long ago, Dr. Fox shared a statistic that has continued to cause me distress. He said that fully one-third of the world's population has never heard the gospel of Jesus Christ. He said that another third have not heard it adequately to make a faith response to Jesus.

And I was convicted! What am I doing to serve Christ in spreading the Good News of the Kingdom? What is my church doing? In a world where 3800 people receive Christ every hour, in a world where ten new churches are started every hour, what are we doing?

And if we are not doing enough, why not? Now I have the answer. It has to do with servanthood. It has to do with denying ourselves for the sake of others. It has to do with humbling ourselves, dying to self, taking up the cross and following Jesus.

The reason we do not have a greater impact on the world is we are unwilling to completely and whole-heartedly surrender to the Lordship of Jesus.

We are a lot like the story about Tommy LaSorda, former manager of the Los Angeles Dodgers. Lasorda accepted a fee to wear a certain shoe a few years back when the Dodgers were in the World Series. Then another manufacturer made a similar offer, and now he had a problem. How could he wear both? He thought maybe he could wear one brand at home and the other on the road and get two fees, but neither company would go for that.

Finally, he figured out a way to get both fees. He simply wore one shoe from each manufacturer.

Many of us would like to do the same thing. Wear one shoe of loyalty to Christ and one shoe of loyalty to self. In fact, a house divided against itself cannot stand. As Jesus said, "No one can serve two masters. Either you will hate one and love the other, or you will be devoted to one and despise the other. You cannot serve both God and money," (Matthew 6:24).

Too many of us have not had the mind of Christ. We have had our own mind, our own will, our own way. And the call of the Gospel is the call to humility and surrender to the Lordship of Christ.

There is a world that is dying, without hope, lost and undone, waiting for the people of God to have the mind that was in Christ Jesus,

> "Who, being in very nature God, did not consider equality
> with God something to be used to his own advantage;
> rather, he made himself nothing by taking the very nature of
> a servant, being made in human likeness.
> And being found in appearance as a man, he humbled himself
>   by becoming obedient to death--even death on a cross!"
> (Philippians 2, 6-8).

I have been a member of the North Georgia Conference of the United Methodist Church of the past 36 years. For almost every one of those years at our annual meeting we have debated our church's stand and that of our nation on the issue of abortion. We have debated, we have passed resolutions, we have sent letters, we have pontificated and often become exasperated. But we have seldom, as far as I know, saved the life of one unwanted child through our ministries with unwed mothers.

However, a few years ago, Carolyn Bransby came to me and told me she wanted to do something to help with the plight of girls with unwanted pregnancies and the babies they so often choose to abort. So we formed a task force to study what we could do. The Beacon of Hope Women's Center is the result of that study.

Carolyn was the founding Executive Director of the Center. She left her good-paying job and took on the mammoth task of running the center. It was the only Crisis Pregnancy Center affiliated with a church in the entire city of Atlanta. Carolyn was a critical part of caring for several girls who made bad decisions or were the victims of violence. She was also responsible for saving the lives of several babies that would have been discarded in the incinerator had she not heard the call of God upon her life and said, "I surrender all." Not only have lives been saved, but some have come to know Christ because she has been willing to have the mind of Christ and humble herself as Jesus humbled himself.

There is a whole world that needs to know Jesus. People are hurting and lives are being destroyed. Sin runs rampant in our nation and around the world. Homes are broken. Children are raised on the trash-heaps of this culture. Young people have no direction for their lives.

Who will be like Jesus? Who will die to self? Will you?

UNDERSTAND WHO JESUS IS.

UNDERSTAND WHAT HE HAS DONE IN OUR BEHALF.

UNDERSTAND THE APPROPRIATE RESPONSE ON OUR PART TO WHO CHRIST IS AND WHAT HE HAS DONE.

Chapter 10

Jesus Rose From The Dead
Luke 24:1-12

Luke 24:1 On the first day of the week, very early in the morning, the women took the spices they had prepared and went to the tomb. 2 They found the stone rolled away from the tomb, 3 but when they entered, they did not find the body of the Lord Jesus. 4 While they were wondering about this, suddenly two men in clothes that gleamed like lightning stood beside them. 5 In their fright the women bowed down with their faces to the ground, but the men said to them, "Why do you look for the living among the dead? 6 He is not here; he has risen! Remember how he told you, while he was still with you in Galilee: 7 `The Son of Man must be delivered into the hands of sinful men, be crucified and on the third day be raised again.'" 8 Then they remembered his words. 9 When they came back from the tomb, they told all these things to the Eleven and to all the others. 10 It was Mary Magdalene, Joanna, Mary the mother of James, and the others with them who told this to the apostles. 11 But they did not believe the women, because their words seemed to them like nonsense. 12 Peter, however, got up and ran to the tomb. Bending over, he saw the strips of linen lying by themselves, and he went away, wondering to himself what had happened.

*****

Why is this story about Jesus in the Bible? Ever wonder about that? Oh, I guess it is easier to answer the question on Easter than on most other days. But, I wonder, not only why this story of Jesus is in the Bible, but also a lot of other stories.

Why is the story of Zaccheaus in the Bible? You remember that story, don't you? Jesus was going into Jericho and a little man, a tax collector named Zaccheaus, wanted to see this famous preacher. But he was too short. So he climbed a sycamore tree just to get to see him. And Jesus saw him up a tree and said, "Zaccheaus, come down, I'm going to your house for lunch." You remember the story. His whole life was changed. Why is that story from the life of Jesus in the Bible?

Why is the story of the lame man at the pool of Bethesda in the Bible? He had been lame for 38 years and for 38 years had existed by having someone carry him to the pool every day where he begged for money to buy bread. One day Jesus came to the pool of Bethesda and saw him there. He healed him and sent him on his way. Why is that story from the life of Jesus in the Bible?

Why is the story of blind Bartimaeus in the Bible? You remember him. He was sitting by the side of the road begging when he heard that Jesus was going to pass by. He yelled, "Jesus, Son of David, have mercy on me!" And Jesus restored his sight. Why is that story from the life of Jesus in the Bible?

Why is the story of the disciples and Jesus in the boat on the Sea of Galilee in the Bible? You remember the story. They were going across the Sea of Galilee one night and a sudden storm came up. They were terrified while Jesus slept soundly in the bow of the boat. They awakened him and he spoke to the winds and the waves and said, "Peace, be still." And the storm disappeared. Why is that story from the life of Jesus in the Bible?

Why is the story of the crazy man of Gerasene in the Bible? You remember the story. He was so crazy that they couldn't even keep him in chains. He roamed naked through the city's cemetery making quite a nuisance of himself. Until the day Jesus came there. He cast the demons out of the man and when the people from the city saw him, he was clothed and in his right mind. Why is that story from the life of Jesus in the Bible?

You remember the story of Jesus feeding the 5000 using only the lunch of one little boy - 5 loaves and 2 fish. Why is that story from the life of Jesus in the Bible?

Do you remember the story of the crucifixion? Jesus was nailed to a cross, but he was not alone. No, there were two other people crucified that day - two thieves. One of them said to Jesus, "Remember me when you come into your kingdom." And Jesus said, "Today you will be with me in Paradise." Why is that story from the life of Jesus in the Bible?

He healed the sick, he restored blind eyes, he made the lame to walk, he set the captive free, he fed the multitudes, he forgave sinners, he stilled the stormy seas, he welcomed thieves into his kingdom.

That is what he did. Not only that, but the most important thing he did was to conquer death. He met the last enemy face to face and was the first person ever to defeat death. He rose from the dead. He was resurrected. That was then. This is now.

Isn't that what Easter is all about? No! If all you understand of the Easter story is that Jesus was raised from the dead you have missed the most important part of the story. The great affirmation of Easter is not that there is an empty tomb, or that Jesus defeated death. No, the great affirmation of Easter is: HE IS ALIVE!

Wow! That changes everything. Suddenly we are not talking about wonderful, but rather dated facts. This thing is not just about what happened 2000 years ago. We do not commemorate Easter.

We do not remember Easter. We do not memorialize Easter. We do not even romanticize Easter. We experience Easter!

Yes, we believe in the historical fact of the resurrection. We also believe in the stories from the life of Jesus. But all those stories and the greatest story of all - Easter - take on all new meaning in light of the resurrection.

Jesus did not just open blind eyes - he still does!

Jesus did not just heal the sick - he still does!

Jesus did not just feed the hungry - he still does!

Jesus did not just transform sinners - he still does!

Jesus did not just still the storms - he still does!

Jesus did not just restore sanity - he still does!

Jesus did not just come back from the grave - he still is alive!

What difference does it all make? All the difference in the world. We are not just commemorating wonderful historical events, we are in the presence of the Risen Savior. Just as surely as Mary Magdalene and Mary, the mother of James, and Joanna came into his presence in the cemetery, he is present here with us.

Did you say, "I don't see him? If I could see him like Mary did, then I might believe all this stuff. But I don't see him."

Don't feel bad. You are in good company. When the disciples first saw the resurrected Jesus, they believed, but not Thomas. He was not there. He said, "Unless I see the nail marks in his hands and put my finger where the nails were, and put my hand into his side, I will not believe," (John 20:25).

But he did later get to see Jesus along with about 500 people, according to Paul. So it's easy to see how those 500 could believe. But what about the billions of people since then who have never seen the resurrected Jesus? Yet they have believed. Are they all just naive, ignorant, easily duped fools?

What is it that could cause mothers to call on his name in the middle of the night when their little baby is so sick that it looks like it may not make it 'til morning?

What is it that could cause a child of 8 or 10 years old to say that she is going to live her whole life telling people about Jesus and then proceed to do just that?

What is it that could cause a young couple to give away 20 or 30 percent of their income just so others may come to know Jesus as Savior and Lord?

What could cause blacks and whites and browns and reds and yellows and all shades in between to love one another?

What is it that would cause a grieving mother and father to stand by the freshly dug grave of their son and know with absolute certainly that they will see him again?

Don't you see? Look around you in the church. There are some folks sitting near you in church who were as good as dead. There was nothing to live for. The answer appeared to be down the wrong end of a loaded .38. But they have been delivered. They have been set free. They have found new life in Jesus Christ.

There are some people in the church who believed the lie of our culture that says, "The more you get the happier you will be." Well, they got it. And you know what? They didn't get happier. No, life only got worse. Broken homes, broken promises, broken lives, broken dreams. Then they met Jesus. They have found meaning and purpose for the first time in their lives.

There are some people in the church who heard the doctors say, "There's nothing more we can do." But they turned to the Great Physician and he healed them and they are alive today because He is alive!

Don't you see? The power of the resurrection is not just in rolling back the heavy stone from the door of the tomb. The power of the resurrection is not just in the testimony of the empty tomb. The power of the resurrection is not just in the testimony of the 500 or so who saw the resurrected Lord. The power of the resurrection is not just in that first Easter.

The power of the resurrection is in the reality of his presence today. He is alive! And just as he opened blind eyes, and healed the sick and fed the multitudes and calmed the storms then - he still does!

I wonder. Have you ever experienced the power of the resurrected Christ? Have you called on him in the middle of the night? Have you experienced his healing? Have you become a new person because he is alive? Have you been delivered from some trap of sin or addiction because he is alive? Have you ever experienced his provision for you when you had nowhere else to turn - did he multiply your loaves and fish? Have you stood at the side of a newly dug grave with grief and absolute confidence because he is alive?

I wonder what kind of witness we could give to those who believe in the historical fact of the resurrection, but have no experience of the resurrected Lord in their lives? I wonder what kind of testimony we could give to those who aren't quite sure that Jesus is alive and changing lives?

I know. What if each one of us who has experienced the power of the resurrection told someone? What if each one of us who knows Jesus just told someone? What if each one of us who has found new life in Christ just told someone? What if each one of us who has been delivered from some life-threatening addiction, disease or dilemma just told someone? What if each one of us who has had the heavy burden of guilt lifted from our backs by the resurrected Lord just told someone?

What if those of us who have experienced the power of the resurrection just told someone and witnessed to the reality that "He is alive!?"

Can I get a witness?

Jesus is alive!   *Hallelujah!*
Jesus is alive!   *Hallelujah!*
Jesus is alive! *Hallelujah!*
Amen.

Chapter 11

Jesus Witnessed to the Perseverance of Grace
Luke 15:1-7

Luke 15:1 Now the tax collectors and "sinners" were all gathering
around to hear him. 2 But the Pharisees and the teachers of the
law muttered, "This man welcomes sinners and eats with them." 3
Then Jesus told them this parable: 4 "Suppose one of you has a
hundred sheep and loses one of them. Does he not leave the ninety-
nine in the open country and go after the lost sheep until he finds
it? 5 And when he finds it, he joyfully puts it on his shoulders 6
and goes home. Then he calls his friends and neighbors together
and says, `Rejoice with me; I have found my lost sheep.' 7 I tell
you that in the same way there will be more rejoicing in heaven
over one sinner who repents than over ninety-nine righteous
persons who do not need to repent.

*****

The first baptism I ever performed was for an 88 year old man in
Stanton, Ky. In Eastern Kentucky, the tradition was baptism by
immersion. Since he was so old and we couldn't baptize him in
the frigid waters of the Red River and since the Methodist Church
did not have a baptistry, we borrowed the Church of Christ
sanctuary one late fall Sunday afternoon in 1972. Our church
arranged to baptize Mr. Everman with me acting as the pastor.
Several men lowered him into the pool and two of us lowered him
into the water while I baptized him in the name of the Father, Son
and Holy Spirit. It had to be one of the most memorable baptisms
of my life.

But what was even more memorable was the story of Mr. Everman's salvation. For most of his life, he had been the lost sheep of his family. Drinking, gambling, carousing, fighting, cheating, lying and stealing were the achievements of his life. For as long as they lived, his parents prayed for the salvation of their lost boy. Aunts and uncles prayed for him. As the older generation died off, nieces and nephews prayed for him. Then when he was old and infirm, his great niece, Wilma, began to care for him. She had prayed for her great uncle, the lost sheep of her family, as long as she could remember. As she cared for him, she shared with him just how much Jesus loved him. He gave his heart to Christ on his 88th birthday – hence the memorable baptism.

It occurs to me that Mr. Everman was the kind of person with whom Jesus spent much of his time; the lost ones of his culture. Luke calls them tax collectors and "sinners." This proclivity of Jesus to hang around such undesirable characters caused the respectable folks of the community to be upset with him. So he told them a parable, a story. It is the story of the lost sheep, the story you read just a moment ago.

The parable is so simple, I will not insult you with giving it an interpretation. 100 sheep; 1 lost; The shepherd seeks after it until he finds it; Brings it home and throws a party. That is the story.

However there is one aspect to the story we may have some trouble understanding. That is the part about the sheep. Very few of us are familiar with sheep. We know dogs, cats, birds and fish, maybe hamsters and iguanas, but very little about sheep.

There is something unusual about sheep. Unlike other animals they do not often deliberately run away. A dog who wants to be free, given a chance, will leave, just like that. A pig or cow will do the same. But sheep do not. They only wander away. They do not mean to. They just drift away without realizing it.

Thus Jesus has deliberately chosen an animal which represents people who are lost, but who never intended to be lost. They never meant to be, and they don't know how it happened. In complete sincerity of purpose they suddenly find themselves lost, and they do not know how it came about.

And so, in using the sheep as the animal in the story, Jesus chooses an animal whose behavior most resembles ours. As a matter of fact, most people who are lost did not intentionally get lost. It just happened. Either they were not properly watched, nurtured, and cared for, or they just lost their way along the way of life.

In October of 2011, several people got lost in a corn maze and had to call 911. They did go to the maze intending to get lost. They just wandered around until it began to dawn on them they were lost and unable to get themselves out of the mess they were in and night was fast approaching.

Like people lost in a corn maze, I have known very few lost folks who intentionally got spiritually lost. Now what do I mean by lost? I mean away from God, lost in the maze of self-absorption, self-indulgence, and self-sufficiency. These are people who find themselves without a personal relationship with God and in the times of honest reflection admit to lives of meaningless pursuits and unfulfilled dreams. Often they have traveled far and fast, and only lately realized they were lost.

Perhaps that describes you. Perhaps more of your life is made up of questions rather than answers, ambiguity rather than assurance. Perhaps you look around where you are and wonder deep in your soul, "How did I ever get here? I didn't start out to be here. But here I am, lost and alone."

Well, I've got some good news for you. Jesus loves lost folks. And this parable is his story to illustrate his love for those who, while they never intended to get lost, find themselves away from the heart of God.

In this parable Jesus tells us something very important about his view of God and humankind. Humankind is represented by the lost sheep. Humankind away from the Good Shepherd is lost. The shepherd reveals God's love for lost humanity.

These are two or three aspects of God's love revealed in this parable that I want to look at this morning.

I. God's love is a seeking love.

Jesus said the shepherd leaves the 99 sheep and goes seeking after one that is lost until he finds it.

God's love seeks us out where ever we are. God's love has been seeking for you. Where has the love of God sought you?

- What about your home? Did you have a mother or a father that revealed to you the truth of God's love for you?

- In school, did you have a saintly teacher that took the time to tell you the story of Jesus and to show you love and compassion?

- Did you grow up in a church where someone shared the story of Jesus with you? Perhaps it was a Sunday school teacher, a youth worker, or a pastor.

- Or maybe you were in the service of your country when you became aware of God's love seeking after you. An officer, or a Chaplain ministered to you in the midst of your fear and anxiety.

When I was pastor of the Trinity United Methodist Church in Covington, Georgia I was making calls on some of my members. I went to the home of an elderly couple and knocked on the door. The lady of the house came to the door but when she saw me she turned away, crying and went back into one of the rooms of the house. (She wasn't the first woman to look at me and cry) I started to turn around and leave but her husband came to the door and invited me in. We walked to the back of the house in silence. I had the feeling I had come during a time of tragedy. It was a long time before anything was said. Finally Mrs. Kendrick came into the room with a letter in her hand. I assumed it contained news of a death of a loved one.

She sat down across from me and smiled through her tears and said, "Preacher, I am so glad you've come, I've just got to tell someone." Then she began to tell me the story of a rebellious and wayward grandson who had been permanently expelled from High School and had been in trouble with the law. It seems that young man had joined the army and was later sent to England. While in England he had become very despondent and lonely. His commanding officer had noticed a change in attitude and began to counsel him. This officer just happened to be a Christian. This young soldier boy was converted and wrote his grandmother to tell her the good news. A portion of the letter said, " I have come all the way to England just to hear that God loves me."

God's love is a seeking love and He is seeking after you.

II. Secondly, God's love is an individual kind of love

Jesus said the shepherd "goes after that which was lost." He does not look for just any sheep. He seeks after that one lost sheep. God, the God that knows folk's name, loves you, *yes you*. Charles Wesley said, "Amazing love, how can it be that thou my God shouldst die for me?"

Karl Barth was perhaps the greatest theologian of the first half of the last century. He wrote monumental volumes on many aspects of Christology. One day he had finished giving a lecture at a German University and was answering questions. Someone asked, "Dr. Barth, what is the most profound truth you have discovered in your theological studies?" Without pausing a moment, the theologian is reported to have said, "That Jesus loves me, this I know, for the Bible tells me so."

My father was in Crawford Long Hospital several years ago and I was visiting him. He told me that a cousin was in a room on the floor below and he called him to come up and meet me. This man, my cousin, came into the room and Daddy introduced me and told him I was the preacher in the family. Then he said "Harold, tell him what happened to you."

Harold said, "Well, your Daddy knows that I have not always lived the way I should. One night I was at home all by myself and couldn't sleep, so I got up and turned on the TV. I had never seen the program that was on so I decided to watch. It turned out to be a religious program. As I sat there listening to that program and it was if someone said to me, "Harold, I love you." I even looked around to see if there was anyone else in the room with me. Then I heard it again, but I knew it was coming from within. "Harold, I love you." As I sat there I realized that God loved me and gave his son to die for me. I accepted Jesus as my savior that night and I've not been the same since."

God's love seeks us out individually and says, "I love you"

III. Thirdly, God's love is patient

Jesus said the shepherd seeks after the lost sheep until he finds it.

Paul wrote about the God of patience. How often we try the patience of God.

Calvary was humankind's slap in the face of God's love. We said:
- God does not really love us
- Jesus is not God's son
- I will not allow myself to be loved.

But God still loves. Even on the cross Jesus prayed, "Father, forgive them."

However, we often try the patience of God's love. I grew up in a grocery store run by my father and his brother. Herbert, my uncle, was a man with a lot of problems. I remember him putting lighter fluid on the shell of my pet turtle and setting it on fire. The turtle wasn't burned but I sure was mad.

Herbert also had a problem with alcohol and drugs. I didn't know about that until I was in High School. He never went to church except for a funeral. His mother and father were both devout Christians and grieved for their wayward son. When Herbert was 61 years old his alcohol and drug problem became so severe he had to be admitted to an institution. While there he was soundly converted and accepted Christ as his Savior. He came home a changed man.

I will always remember him telling me that Jesus had saved him from his sins. There was a peace and joy in his face that had never been there before. Herbert was killed in an accident not long after that, but I expect to see him in heaven. This man spent 61 years trying the patience of God, yet God never stopped loving him and God never stopped seeking him.

How long have you been trying God's patience?
He still loves you. He always will.

The church under the loving care of Jesus, the Good Shepherd, is the world's lost and found department, seeking out for rescue the lost, the strayed or the stolen.

Remember:
God's love is a seeking kind of love;
God's love is an individual kind of love;
God's love is a patient kind of love.

If you are aware of your need to accept the love of God, you may do so even now, by opening your life to Him.

All you have to do is say:

Lord Jesus, I need your love in me
I am lost and astray
Fill my heart with your love and presence.

Accept His presence by faith and live by faith.

Chapter 12

Jesus Called for Perfection
Matthew 5:43-48

Matthew 5:43 "You have heard that it was said, `Love your neighbor and hate your enemy.' 44 But I tell you: Love your enemies and pray for those who persecute you, 45 that you may be sons of your Father in heaven. He causes his sun to rise on the evil and the good, and sends rain on the righteous and the unrighteous. 46 If you love those who love you, what reward will you get? Are not even the tax collectors doing that? 47 And if you greet only your brothers, what are you doing more than others? Do not even pagans do that? 48 Be perfect, therefore, as your heavenly Father is perfect.

*****

On the Sundays I am in the United States I get to preach at the Due West United Methodist Church in western Cobb County, GA. It is a very large church with some remarkable ministries. I have observed them as the church has grown through the years. I observed them as an occasional consultant to their leaders. I observed them as I served as their District Superintendent. I have observed them as I have worked with some of their leaders both here and in Venezuela. However, I know very little of the whole of how this church is touching the lives of so many in this community. Lives are being transformed by the grace of Jesus through the ministries of the Due West Church – and I celebrate that with them – even though I know very few of the actual stories.

And most of the members of Due West only know a little of the story of grace being played out in that church. Why? Because God is at work through so many different ways in this congregation, no one knows them all – not even the pastor, Dr. Tom Davis! My good friend, Dr. John Ed Mathison, used to say that if the pastor knew everything going on in the church, not enough was going on in the church. God's grace is reaching out to people in ways we cannot even imagine.

I remember a staff retreat when I was the Senior Minister of a large church in Alpharetta. The staff was celebrating many of the ways God was working in that congregation.

However, the story I remember best was one I had not heard and did not know until it was shared by one of the ministers, Rev. Mike Roper. Mike is the finest Minister of Caring I know in the United Methodist Church.

The story Mike told was of a Muslim woman who came to the church for help after being abandoned and divorced by her husband who returned to their home country and left her and their child in a foreign land. She was sick, broke, had no marketable skills and spoke very little English. She knew very little of our culture or customs. She needed lots of help.

Through the Counseling Center, the Caring Ministry, the Christian School, and a vast number of lay care givers, she received significant help for some very difficult problems in her life. Then one day she showed up at our Caring Minister's office to thank him for all the help she had received from the congregation.

But there was more. Her curiosity had not been satisfied. She simply had to know why? Why had so many people loved her, people who did not know her? Why had so many taken time out of their busy day to drive her to multiple appointments? Why had so many reached out to her with obvious love and in sacrificial service? Why had so many people given her food and clothes and furniture and a hundred other things. Why?

Mike proceeded to explain to her why this had happened. He told her it was because of Jesus. He told her these people had received such love from Jesus that they just had to share it. He asked her if she would like to know Jesus. She eagerly asked Jesus to come in to her heart as she gave her life to Christ. And that is what Jesus was talking about in today's Scripture Reading. Hear it again:

Matthew 5:43 "You have heard that it was said, 'Love your neighbor and hate your enemy.' 44 But I tell you: Love your enemies and pray for those who persecute you, 45 that you may be sons of your Father in heaven. He causes his sun to rise on the evil and the good, and sends rain on the righteous and the unrighteous. 46 If you love those who love you, what reward will you get? Are not even the tax collectors doing that? 47 And if you greet only your brothers, what are you doing more than others? Do not even pagans do that? 48 Be perfect, therefore, as your heavenly Father is perfect."

Jesus was saying we are to love people who are not like us, people who are not close to us, people who hurt us, people who see themselves as our enemies and even people who hate us. That is a pretty tall order.

Let's deal with the most difficult first. We are to love people who hate us. Jesus said, "You have heard it said, 'Love your neighbor and hate your enemy.'" That makes perfect sense doesn't? Love those who are like you, who live like you, who treat you fairly and equitably.

Makes sense. But what is this nonsense about loving your enemies? Jesus said, "But I tell you: Love your enemies and pray for those who persecute you…"Now why would he say something like that? It goes against everything in us. We do not naturally love our enemies. No, naturally we want to get them back, to retaliate, to get even.

And we will go to some pretty bizarre lengths to treat our enemies that way we think they ought to be treated. We want to treat our enemies in a way that exacts retribution upon them. We want them to pay. We want them to suffer because of what they have done to us. It is the way of the world. It is the natural order of things. But Jesus said, "Love your enemies and pray for them." What kind of nonsense is that? Why would he say such a thing? How are we supposed to accomplish that?

Jesus gives two explanatory notes that explain such a strange idea, an idea like loving your enemy. The first one is: "He causes his sun to rise on the evil and the good, and sends rain on the righteous and the unrighteous." The second one is: "Be perfect, therefore, as your heavenly Father is perfect." The first one sums up grace: "He causes his sun to rise on the evil and the good and sends rain on the righteous and the unrighteous."

This describes the nature of God. For God is a holy and righteous God. Yet this Holy God is impartial in the grace he freely bestows on all, both saints and sinners, or righteous and unrighteous. God's grace is freely given to all people, even to those people who are his sworn enemies, such as the ones who nailed Jesus to the cross or the ones who today take His name in vain. The rain of grace falls on the good and the bad. The warm sunshine of God's love shines on the evil and the good. To love your enemies and pray for them is the Godly thing to do. It is not the worldly thing to do, it is the Godly thing to do.

But why? Why should we do that? What is the reason for Jesus telling us to love our enemies? I think there are several, but the one I want us to focus on this morning is the reason of grace. For as we come to understand grace, we begin to understand that we are the recipients of God's unmerited favor. That glorious grace has made a provision whereby we can be forgiven of our sins and restored into a right relationship with God. We who were sinners and alienated from God have received the grace of God and have been saved from our sins. We who were lost are found. We who are unrighteous have received the righteousness of Christ.

As a result of that wonderful experience of grace, we become aware that God's grace is given to all, just as it was to us. Yes, we had to respond to the grace. But it was by grace that we were able to respond. Others may have not yet responded to God's grace in their lives, but God's gracious rain still falls on them and God's gracious sun still shines on them. Therefore, who are we to stand in judgment of anyone by returning hate with hate? If God has loved them with an everlasting love why shouldn't we, we who have been the recipients of the same grace Jesus tells us to show to them?

Why don't we love our enemies? Even if we understand that we ought to love them we find that we cannot. For their treatment of us or those whom we love precludes us from loving them in the way Jesus tells us to love them. Jesus knew that. That is why He gave us the secret to loving our enemies. The secret is: "Pray for them." That's right, He said, "Love your enemies and pray for them."

We get so hung up on the seemingly impossible command to love our enemies, we forget the rest of it, the "how" of it. We love our enemies by praying for them. Oh, this is not easy, but it is possible. You can consciously add the name of your enemy to your prayer list and at least daily pray for them. I am here to tell you if you do that and stick with praying for your enemy, you will eventually discover that you love your enemy.

If you don't believe it, try praying for your spouse and see how much more you begin to love him or her after you have prayed for them daily for a while. You pray for your enemies' best interest, you pray for their success, you pray for their salvation, you pray for their family, you pray for their work, your pray for their vacation, you pray for them and over time you will discover that you love them. Jesus guarantees it.

So Jesus' first explanatory note on loving your enemies is the note concerning the universality of grace in rain and sun being given to all, regardless of merit. The second explanatory note is even more difficult for us to understand: "Be perfect as your heavenly father is perfect." Just as we have excused ourselves from the requirement of loving our enemies because it is not natural, so we have also excused ourselves from this word of Jesus because we think it is utterly impossible.

"Be perfect." Now whoever heard such a ridiculous idea? Perfect? "No one is perfect," we say. "We all make mistakes," we say. "There's only been one perfect man," we say. So we skip over these words of Jesus. Why? Because we do not understand them and we do not believe them to be possible or practical. W

Perhaps we need to understand them better. What does Jesus mean by "perfect?" Simply defined the word would be "whole or complete." Jesus wants us to experience wholeness, perfection.

We are moving into apple season in North Georgia. Ever seen a perfect apple? Of course you have. It is one without rot or disease or deformity. It is whole. Go to the store today and you can see dozens of perfect apples. That doesn't mean they are all the same. It simply means they have apple integrity, they exhibit wholeness. "There ain't no worms in a perfect apple."

And one of the worms Jesus wants to eliminate from our lives is the worm of hate. He tells us how to get rid of it, then he tells us why. He wants us to be perfect, whole. But you say, "I am not perfect. I am not whole." If you were would it have been so important to Jesus to speak the obvious or unnecessary? He knows you are not perfect, he knows you are not whole. If you were it would have been unnecessary for him to have just given you instructions on how to love your enemies.

It is because you are not perfect or whole that Jesus said, "Be perfect." You see we are to aim for perfection. But you say, "I may not reach absolute perfection." Maybe not, but you will never get even close if you do not aim for it. If you aim for imperfection, you will hit it every time. There is no challenge in that. There is no growth in that. There is nothing lofty in that.

One of the questions John Wesley asked all his preachers before they were ordained and still asked of all United Methodist preachers today is, "Do you expect to be made perfect in this life?" We all have to answer "Yes."

You know preachers. Have we attained it? Of course not. But it must be our aim or we will settle for the mediocrity of excuses and comparisons. You will note that Jesus was specific. He said, "Be perfect as your father in heaven is perfect. There is no room for comparison with others around us. The standard is God, Himself.

Followers of Christ are people who are going on to perfection. The pursuit of perfection is lived out in how we love and treat our enemies. And how we love and treat our enemies is fueled by and informed by the stark reality of the universality of God's grace, grace that included you and me and includes our enemies.

After all, this is all about grace – grace given to the friends of God and the enemies of God, but freely given nevertheless. "Be perfect even as your Father in heaven is perfect." Are you, "Going on to perfection?" Are you becoming more and more like Jesus? Is your life one of complete wholeness and moral and ethical integrity. Do people take notice of you that "you have been with Jesus?" Is love your aim? Are you being made perfect in love?

The fact that you probably answered, "No," to one of the above questions is the result of the work of grace in your life whereby the Spirit is drawing you forward into a life of surrender and holiness before the Lord. Pray for the Spirit to complete the work of redemption in you. Pray for that now.

And "Be perfect as your father in heaven is perfect."